GRACED TO GOVERN

IMPACTING A GENERATION
LEADERSHIP ANTHOLOGY

DR. DEBORAH C. ANTHONY
FOUNDING AUTHOR

GRACED TO GOVERN
Impacting A Generation

Dr. Deborah C. Anthony
deborah@deborahcanthony.com

ISBN 978-1-943343-19-5

Printed in the USA.

Published by: Destined To Publish | Flossmoor, Illinois
www.DestinedToPublish.com

DEDICATION

You Are Graced to Impact

This volume is dedicated to the generations who will come after us those who will one day open these pages and find undeniable evidence that God was present in our time: speaking, shaping, healing, building, and calling His people forward through the lives and testimonies of these writers.

It is dedicated to the Baby Boomers, Generation X, Millennials, Generation Z, and Generation Alpha and to the generations still unfolding in the providence of God. My prayer is that my children, your children, and our children's children will know the Lord not as a distant idea, but as a living reality personally encountered, deeply trusted, and faithfully followed.

And over every reader, every household, and every bloodline represented, I speak the Abrahamic blessing: that God would establish His covenant, enlarge your inheritance, and cause you to walk in divine favor with enduring faith. May He keep His promise to a thousand generations and may what is recorded here serve as both witness and invitation: a witness that God keeps covenant, and an invitation to rise beyond inspiration into obedience.

May our lives, aligned with His purpose, produce fruit that remains leaving generational impact that outlives us and advances the Kingdom long after we are gone. "*Now the Lord had said unto Abram, Get thee out of thy country, and from thy kindred, and from thy father's house, unto a land that I will shew thee: And I will make of thee*

FOREWORD

Prophetess Aqua L. Robins
AUTHOR • COUNSELOR • COACH
H2O Unlimited Hub
MeMatters Counseling & Empowerment Center

In every generation, God raises voices—leaders with wisdom, courage, and vision who guide His people and shape the destiny of nations. *Graced to Govern – Impacting a Generation* gathers those voices for such a time as this. More than testimonies or teachings, this work is a clarion call and a roadmap for anyone seeking to serve with authority rooted in grace, tempered by humility, and sharpened by spiritual discernment.

Too often, leadership is framed by power, platform, or personality. The standard presented here is different: leadership marked by God's grace—His unmerited favor, enabling power, and transforming presence. Across these pages, diverse leaders speak honestly about the joys and costs of governing under God's authority. They offer encouragement and practical wisdom to those entrusted with the sacred work of spiritual leadership—whether in the church, the public square, the marketplace, or the home.

This volume bears a distinct assignment: impacting a generation. It invites fathers and mothers in the faith to labor for legacy;

pastors and public servants to steward people with justice and mercy; educators and entrepreneurs to form culture through truth and excellence; and everyday believers to govern their own spheres—hearts, homes, and hands—with integrity. Here, governance is not control; it brings people, systems, and decisions under the Lordship of Jesus Christ for the good of others.

You will hear echoes of Joseph's administrative grace, Esther's intercessory courage, and Daniel's uncompromised witness. Yet the emphasis is not merely on biblical heroes—it is on becoming that kind of leader for the generation before us and the generation after us. These pages model a leadership that disciples, equips, and deploys; that tells the truth in love; that embraces accountability; and that embraces the next generation with hope.

As you journey through these pages, may you receive fresh courage, deeper understanding, and a renewed sense of calling. May grace train your hands to build, your heart to intercede, and your voice to speak life. And may this book activate you to do more than admire Kingdom leadership—to embody it so that children, families, churches, and communities encounter the living God through leaders who govern well.

It is my prayer that *Graced to Govern – Impacting a Generation* ignites a movement of Kingdom-minded leaders—women and men clothed with grace, seasoned by wisdom, and steadfast in faith—who will govern their spheres for the glory of God and the good of humanity. May you be equipped, inspired, and transformed as you read, and may your life become another strong voice in the chorus of Kingdom leaders—for this generation and for those to come.

TABLE OF CONTENTS

SECTION IV: KINGDOM GOVERNANCE

SECTION V: SPHERES OF IMPACT

SECTION VI: HEALING & IDENTITY

SECTION VII: THE BLESSING OF IMPACT

INTRODUCTION

Impacting a Generation

Dr. Deborah C. Anthony
FOUNDING AUTHOR

There is an urgency in the earth, a holy stirring that reminds us how imperative it is that we leave a mark—an indelible impact—on the generation before us and the generations rising after us. Every time I think about Joshua, a great leader and mighty man of valor, I am arrested by the sobering truth recorded just a few verses after his death:

> *"And also all that generation were gathered unto their fathers: and there arose another generation after them, which knew not the LORD ..."* (Judges 2:10).

After all the miracles of coming out of Egypt, after all that God had done for His people, after all the wonders they witnessed with their own eyes—how does a generation arise that knows not the God of their fathers?

How does a people forget the God who parted the Red Sea?

The God who fed them with manna?

The God who caused walls to fall and enemies to flee?

It happens when voices fall silent.

It happens when stories go untold.

It happens when the legacy of righteousness is not intentionally imparted.

This is why *Graced to Govern – Impacting a Generation (Series Two)* exists.

This collaboration of authors is not simply a collection of writings.

It is a movement, a mantle, a mandate to ensure that the God of our fathers is known by our sons and daughters.

We are living in the greatest time in human history, where information travels at the speed of light, where geographical borders cannot mute the Gospel, and where technology places truth into the hands of people across the world in an instant. If ever there was a moment for the voices of the seasoned, the silenced, the overlooked, the Baby Boomers, the Silent Generation, and those who have faithfully served in the shadows, it is now.

Their wisdom cannot be buried.

Their stories cannot be lost.

Their impact cannot be erased.

I am committed through these *Graced to Govern* series to ensuring that the voices of those who paved the way—those who prayed, labored, built, sacrificed, and stood for righteousness—are amplified throughout all twelve realms of influence. These are the voices that leave a legacy. These are the voices that plant seeds of faith, conviction, and courage in the earth—seeds that must bring forth fruit that remains until the return of our Lord Jesus Christ.

This is the Kingdom as she prepares for the Bridegroom.

I cannot write this introduction without honoring the man whose shoulders I stand upon—my grandfather, Rev. Hiram Crawford. A true prophet of his generation. A builder in both the natural and the spirit. A man of unshakeable vision who believed in the power of education, the necessity of business, and the absolute priority of standing on the right side of God and His Kingdom.

I pick up the torch of my grandfather and countless others who cried aloud in their day, "Prepare ye the way of the Lord." I echo that same cry in mine. Our impact on this generation must be more than eloquent words—it must be marked by power, by presence, and by prayer that shifts atmospheres, transforms hearts, and establishes righteousness in the land.

It must be legacy.

It must be intentional.

It must be eternal.

Welcome to *Impacting a Generation*—Series Two of the *Graced to Govern* collective.

May every page stir you.

May every story awaken you.

May every author ignite something in you that will outlive your lifetime.

Enjoy each voice.

Honor each journey.

And may the grace to govern rest upon you as you read.

A Final Call to the Reader

> *"If my people, which are called by my name, shall humble themselves, and pray, and seek my face, and turn from their wicked ways; then will I hear from heaven, and will forgive their sin, and will heal their land"* (2 Chronicles 7:14).

Let this scripture awaken something deep within you. Let it call you into alignment with the heart of God. And as you read these pages, ask yourself with honesty and conviction:

"Am I His people?"

Am I one who humbles myself?

Am I one who prays?

Am I one who seeks His face?

Am I one willing to turn so God can heal our land?

Because impacting a generation begins with those who say yes to becoming His people fully, wholly, intentionally, and without hesitation.

FOUNDATION OF IMPACT

1

JOHN BOY'S LEGACY AND THE GENERATION HE IS SHAPING

John Anthony

I never expected the story of my son to reach beyond the walls of our home. I believed his life belonged to the rhythm of our days, to the laughter that moved through our rooms and to the moments only a father remembers in quiet reflection. I did not imagine that his legacy would one day speak to families I have never met. I did not foresee that the love I carried for him would become a source of strength for a generation fighting battles they often keep hidden.

Nothing prepares a parent for that kind of journey. Nothing prepares a father to realize that the story of his child shaped by both beauty and struggle now serves as a guide for people searching for understanding, hope, and clarity.

A Quiet Strength and the Hidden Struggles of Youth

I lived my life beside a young man who carried a warmth that could change the atmosphere of a room the moment he entered it. His smile brought ease. His laughter pulled people closer. He had a presence that made others feel seen, even when he said very little. I watched the way he lifted others without effort, and I admired it.

Yet there were moments when quiet settled around him. There were days when his light dimmed in a way I could not fully name. At the time, I believed these shifts were simply part of growing up. Young people move through many emotional stages, and parents often assume those fluctuations are temporary. I see now that I did not always understand the depth behind those quiet stretches. I did not always grasp the conversations he was having within himself.

I have learned that many children walk through life with a mixture of confidence and doubt. They want to please the people who love them while managing questions they cannot fully express. They want to protect their families from their own sadness. They want to appear strong because they believe strength earns safety.

My son walked this same path. He fought quietly. He wrestled with emotions that gathered slowly rather than arriving with force.

There was nothing dramatic or obvious—only subtle changes that blended into daily life. When I look back, I do not do so with blame. I look back with a clearer understanding of how complicated a young person's heart can be and how important it is for a parent to slow down enough to see what is not easily spoken.

When Grief Becomes Purpose

When I began writing about my son after his passing, I did not expect healing to flow beyond my own grief. I wrote because silence felt unbearable. I wrote because honesty was the only way I knew to honor his life. I wrote because I needed people to understand the weight and beauty of his presence.

What happened next was something I could never have predicted. Parents began reaching out. Young people began sharing their struggles. Families who felt alone discovered that my story reflected their own hidden pain. Through this unexpected response, I realized that my son's life carried a message that extended far beyond my personal sorrow. His legacy began to guide others toward deeper awareness and compassion.

One of the most important truths I have learned is that emotional struggle often enters a home quietly. A child may pull back a little. They may seem tired more often. They may sit in silence where there was once conversation. They may offer a polite smile that fades as soon as the moment passes. These changes do not announce themselves. They drift. They soften. They blend into the background of a busy family. That is what makes them easy to miss.

Parents are not negligent; they are overwhelmed. They are juggling responsibilities, schedules, and concerns of their own. I have lived that reality. I know the weight of it. Yet I also know now that love deepens when awareness expands. When we learn to notice our children with a slower gaze, we begin to understand what their hearts are trying to communicate.

My son's legacy has invited families to take this slower approach. It has encouraged parents to ask gentle questions and to listen without assumption. It has shown them that emotional presence offers safety before any solution ever appears.

I have spoken with countless parents who shared their regrets with tears in their eyes, and I have spoken with others who discovered a new closeness with their children because they began to see them more clearly. Every one of these conversations reminds me that love grows through attention. It grows through quiet observation. It grows when a parent chooses presence over hurry.

The Next Generation: Finding Courage in His Story

Young people who encounter my son's story often respond with an honesty that surprises them. They begin to open their hearts in ways they once avoided. Some of them see themselves in him not because their experiences are identical, but because they understand the tension between outward confidence and private uncertainty.

They find comfort in realizing they are not alone in their silence. They find courage to speak with parents, mentors, or friends. Many have written to me, describing how they shared emotions they once buried. Some have said that opening up saved their lives.

I do not take those words lightly. They reveal the fragile strength young people carry within them. They reveal the impact of a life that continues to guide others toward healing.

Teaching, Healing, and Leading Through Legacy

Teachers and counselors have told me how my son's story has changed the way they approach the students under their care. They have described moments when they noticed a student withdraw and chose patience instead of pressure. They have talked about conversations that would never have happened without the insight they gained through this journey.

They now understand that emotional distress is not always loud. It can be soft. It can hide behind politeness. It can disguise itself as a quiet child who never causes trouble. His legacy has shown them how to look deeper, listen differently, and create space for students still learning to speak their truth.

The influence of his life extends beyond schools into entire communities. Families who once felt isolated in grief have found comfort in knowing others understand their experience. Grief creates a sense of separation that can feel unbearable. It convinces parents that no one else carries a wound like theirs.

When these families encounter my writing, they realize they are not alone. They find a common language for emotions that never fit into ordinary conversations. They find connection. That connection becomes a form of healing. It restores the sense that life can continue with strength and dignity even in the presence of sorrow.

When Fathers Heal

Fathers, in particular, have shared how this journey has transformed them. Many of us grew up believing that emotional restraint was a requirement for manhood. We were taught to be steady, to solve problems without complaint, to hide our fear and grief.

Losing my son shattered that idea by force. I learned that strength is not the absence of emotion. Strength is the willingness to feel. Strength is the courage to speak the truth even when it exposes the most vulnerable parts of the heart.

When fathers encounter my writing, they often say it gives them permission to love their children with more tenderness. They step toward their sons and daughters with deeper vulnerability. They offer affection without hesitation. They become more present in the daily lives of their families. This shift is one of the most beautiful outcomes of my son's legacy.

A Generation Under Pressure

Across the country, young people face pressures that past generations never encountered at this scale. They live in a world of constant comparison. They carry expectations that exceed their emotional resources. They are surrounded by information that overwhelms rather than guides. Many feel lost in a crowd of voices demanding perfection.

My son lived within this same world. His story helps shed light on the weight young people carry. It directs parents to engage more thoughtfully. It invites leaders and mentors to create safe environments for emotional expression. It encourages young people to acknowledge their internal struggles without shame.

As I continue to share his story, I have seen how it shapes the future. The parents who learn from this journey will raise their children with a more attentive heart. They will recognize the early signs of emotional distress. They will create homes where feelings can be expressed without fear. They will teach their children the value of speaking openly.

These families will be stronger because they understand that emotional health is not a luxury, it is essential. It is the foundation upon which resilience is built. Communities influenced by my son's legacy are beginning to embrace a culture of compassion. They check on one another more often. They invest time in conversations that once felt uncomfortable. They recognize that emotional well-being is not only an individual concern but a collective responsibility.

These communities support their young people with greater tenderness. They walk with one another through seasons of difficulty. They become places where healing is possible.

Through all of this, I have learned that a legacy does not depend on the number of years lived. It depends on the depth of love carried and the truth revealed. My son's life holds a message that continues to awaken hearts.

It encourages parents to pause.

It encourages young people to speak.

It encourages communities to care.

It encourages leaders to look beyond the surface.

His story continues to shape the national conversation about emotional health with a clarity that cannot be ignored.

I tell this story because I want parents to see their children through the eyes of presence rather than assumption. I want families to understand that emotional changes in a child deserve attention. I want young people to know that their feelings matter. I want communities to refuse the silence that allows suffering to grow unchecked.

Love is not passive. Love sees. Love listens. Love responds.

The Legacy That Lives On

The legacy of my son is not defined by his passing it is defined by the way his life continues to guide others. It is defined by the comfort his story has brought to families who lost children of their own. It is defined by the courage it has inspired in young people who once believed they had no voice. It is defined by the fathers who now embrace their children with newfound tenderness. It is defined by the conversations that happen in living rooms, classrooms, and communities because his story revealed a truth that many felt but did not know how to express.

His life has become a blessing that reaches across generations. It continues to move with quiet strength through the hearts of people seeking clarity in a complicated world. It continues to build connections between families who might otherwise remain in isolation. It continues to inspire healing in young people who need reassurance that their lives matter beyond measure.

Even in grief, love can expand rather than shrink.

John Boy's Next Chapter From Page to Screen

And now his legacy enters a new chapter. The book I wrote for him, the book that began as a father trying to survive the weight of loss, is being adapted into a film. I never imagined that the pages I wrote through tears would one day rise onto a screen.

Families who may never read the book will encounter his story in theaters and living rooms. This film will reach people searching for answers, for understanding, and for a way to help their children speak the truth of their hearts. It will reach young people who believe their silence has no witness. It will reach parents who fear they have missed something important. It will reach communities that want to understand how to care for those who feel unseen.

A film carries emotion in a way the page never can. It brings breath, movement, and presence to the story of my son. It creates space for people to feel what a family feels when they love a child who struggles. It gives families a place to have conversations they have long avoided.

If this film gives even one young person the courage to speak, or helps even one parent slow down long enough to see what their child cannot say, then my son's story will continue to save lives in ways that go far beyond my reach.

His Legacy, Our Mandate

His legacy will grow because this film will open new doors. It will carry his voice into spaces I could never enter alone. It will remind people that awareness can protect, that compassion can heal, and that love must move at the pace of the heart.

It will show the truth that shaped every word I wrote:

My son mattered. His life mattered.
His story matters still.

This is the legacy of my son a legacy that continues to rise, a legacy that keeps moving into the lives of parents, young people, teachers, leaders, and communities who are searching for hope and truth, a legacy that remains a gift which continues to give now and for generations to come.

John Anthony is a former police officer and Illinois State Representative who now writes and speaks on grief, healing, and emotional awareness. He is the author of *Letters to John Boy* and the radio host of *Detroit Morning Answer*. John is the husband of Dr. Deborah C. Anthony and father to Jada, Kirsten, Kylie, Karis, Joriah, and his late son, John Wesley Christian Anthony. His work offers families clarity, compassion, and hope in navigating life's hidden struggles.

2

THE WEIGHT OF THE BATON

Making the Exchange Count

Dr. Tawanda Barnes Ervin

The movers' boots echoed against the still perfect hardwood floors. Floors I had chosen plank by plank, imagining the sound of my boys running across them. The weather was rather warm for a November day in South Carolina, with a high of 63 degrees. My kids had taken the golf cart for one last spin before it was packed onto the moving truck. Boxes crowded the entryway like silent witnesses to a story that felt unfinished. The scent of cardboard and fresh paint filled the air as they lifted furniture that had barely settled into its rightful place.

Above them, the coffered ceilings caught the afternoon light, a detail I'd once prayed for, pinned, and finally seen come to life. Every beam had felt like a promise fulfilled. Every detail, from the wainscoting to the wide staircase to the soft-close drawers, was born out of vision, prayer, and precision. This home wasn't even two years old.

The open-concept kitchen still carried the warmth of taking on Thanksgiving hosting duties all on my own. The master suite, my sanctuary, held a private den where I wrote, prayed, and dreamed about what was next. Where I worked through late nights uninterrupted, finishing my master's degree while my husband was in another state working. Now, movers lifted furniture from corners that had only just learned our rhythm. With each creak of a dolly and pull of packing tape, I could feel the life we'd built being unstitched.

Remnants of a celebration that doubled as our farewell lingered in the corners. Our family had come two days before to celebrate my son's sixth birthday in advance. We smiled through the uncertainty, masking the ache with laughter.

Six figures to zero. No unemployment, no cushion, just faith. The kind of faith that doesn't always come with explanations.

We were leaving behind a dream home we'd built with strategy and prayer, trading it for a house we had only seen online. No tours. No guarantees. Just a word from God. It didn't make sense to anyone looking in, and, truthfully, it barely made sense to me.

But I knew what this was.

Nobody wanted to leave. But it was a God move.

The Question

Two weeks after we arrived, the call came.

My mother—strong, radiant, my prayer warrior—had been diagnosed with stage three breast cancer. The weight of those words hit harder than any box we had lifted. I had just left everything familiar in obedience only to find myself hundreds of miles away when she needed me most. Within days, COVID hit. Distance turned from inconvenient to dangerous. I couldn't fly home. Couldn't sit with her in chemo. Couldn't wrap my arms around her the way a daughter should.

I wrestled in silence. I had said yes to God, but every headline and every phone call made that yes feel heavier. My faith hadn't failed, but it felt bruised.

Then came 2022. My father, my first pastor, my Blueprint of faith, was diagnosed with cancer too. Caught early, praise God, but still enough to shake me. Yet he never stopped preaching. Never missed a Sunday. Watching him stand behind the pulpit with strength that defied his diagnosis, I saw legacy in motion. His mantle was still falling forward.

I'm the only girl of three, and I'm a die-hard daddy's girl. Now, I found myself asking God the question that had been sitting in my chest for months: "Why do I get to watch legacy exchange when the one You gave me feels interrupted? Why did You have me leave the very ground You told me to build on?"

His answer came quietly, almost like a vision. He showed me the help He had already prepared, including some individuals who would return from another state at just the right time. They joined the faithful team my parents had been nurturing for years.

People who had been positioned and trained and were ready to step up. My parents weren't going to be alone. They were going to be surrounded by the fruit of decades of pouring into others.

In that moment, I understood:

My obedience made room for provision I couldn't see.

What felt like loss was actually God repositioning the pieces.

My surrender created space for others to step into their yes.

What Came Next

The years that followed tested everything I thought I understood about holding and releasing the baton.

They were marked by the kind of seasons that don't announce themselves; they just arrive and rearrange you. One by one, the familiar pillars in my life shifted. Losses I couldn't prevent. Diagnoses I couldn't fix. Grief that stretched across 900 miles, making distance feel heavier than any suitcase we'd ever packed.

But even in that weight, I kept sensing God whispering, "This is still the exchange."

I had always equated faithful service with control, by managing, planning, producing outcomes. But now, stewardship meant surrender. Servanthood meant trusting what I couldn't see and holding sacred what I couldn't hold steady.

I learned to lead in spaces, without certainty. To love without proximity. To build when the Blueprint was blurry.

And somewhere between the pain and the promise, something in me shifted. My faith began to outgrow my trauma. What once felt like fragments started to form a foundation.

The baton didn't slip; it transformed.

I realized that legacy isn't only what you leave behind; it's also what you learn to carry differently.

Every loss, every unanswered question, became a reminder that even in what feels like interruption, God is still writing continuation.

Making the Exchange Count

Obedience will always involve an exchange, something placed in your hands, and something required in return. To make the exchange count, you must learn to discern what's yours to carry, what's yours to release, and when to do both.

1. Discernment: Know What's Yours

   Every baton carries weight, but not every baton carries your assignment.

   Some batons we receive, and others we release. Both require faith. Both require grace. Both require discernment. And both require the wisdom to know which one God is calling you to in this season.

   My father received his father's church, a literal handoff of leadership, calling, and community. I've watched him steward that baton with dignity and longevity, building on what was handed to him with honor while continuing to serve the ministry he was called to as under-shepherd in the '80s.

That's discernment in motion: recognizing a legacy worth continuing and carrying it forward with reverence.

However, discernment doesn't always manifest as inheritance. Sometimes it looks like release. When God told us to leave our ministry, it felt like dropping the baton mid-race. Everything in me wanted to hold tighter, to manage the outcome, to keep the pace, to prove the worth of the work. But in that moment, God wasn't asking me to win the race; He was asking me to trust His route. And I did!

Leaving didn't mean failure. It meant faith.

It meant understanding that obedience sometimes looks like letting go of what once was so that God can multiply it through someone else.

Discernment is the bridge between emotion and obedience. It's learning to recognize God's voice above every other, including your own logic, your family's concern, and your fear of the unknown. It's what allows you to say yes when circumstances scream no. It's the difference between holding on out of fear and releasing out of trust. It asks deeper questions than "Should I stay, or should I go?" It asks, "What is God asking me to do with what's in my hands?"

That question realigns your focus. Because the truth is, the weight of the baton doesn't change; it's what the baton represents that determines how you carry it.

For some, the baton is a business, a ministry, a family name, or a generational vision. For others, it's a calling, a promise, or an unfinished dream. But regardless of the form, every baton has divine timing attached to it.

Discernment keeps you from running ahead of God or lagging behind Him. It teaches you how to move with grace in the transition. It's how you protect the integrity of the exchange, ensuring that what's handed off is healthy, whole, and ready for the next set of hands.

When you know what's yours, you stop comparing your assignment to someone else's. You stop resenting the handoff. You stop trying to hold on to something that grace has already lifted off of you.

The truth is, God doesn't measure your legacy by how long you hold the baton. He measures it by how faithfully you carried it and how obediently you released it.

Discernment keeps your hands light enough to move when He says move and strong enough to hold when He says hold. It turns confusion into clarity and loss into leadership.

So, before you make another move, ask yourself:

- Is this something God is asking me to carry or something He's asking me to complete?
- Am I holding this because I'm called or because I'm comfortable?
- Am I releasing this because I'm tired or because it's time?
- Can I hear God clearly enough to trust His leading, even when the path isn't clear?

When you can answer those questions honestly before God, you'll begin to see the beauty in both receiving and releasing. Both are acts of governance. Both are grace.

2. Obedience Over Opinion

Obedience rarely looks impressive from the outside, and it's even harder when the noise gets loud. To some, my yes looked like abandonment. Leaving my father when he needed help. Closing a ministry still in its infancy. Moving away from family support with two sons on the spectrum. The opinions came from every direction—some whispered, some spoken directly. Well-meaning voices questioned the timing, the wisdom, the cost.

But true obedience isn't about silencing the noise by defending yourself; it's about discerning which voice you're meant to follow. People who love you may not understand your moves. That's the tension of walking by faith; sometimes, the people closest to you can't see what God has shown you.

What looks like a loss in one season is often a sign of positioning for the next. When I began hearing about the help my parents were now receiving, I realized my surrender had made space for their assignment. The noise didn't change God's plan. It just tested whether I would trust His voice above all others.

That's faithful stewardship! "... *commit thou to faithful men*" (2 Timothy 2:2). God doesn't measure your obedience by how many people agree with you. He measures it by whether you moved when He said move.

3. Provision Follows Positioning

You can't always see provision before the move; sometimes it meets you because you moved. When we left, there was no visible safety net, just savings and faith. I couldn't see all of the ways God would send the help for my parents. But obedience positions you for what sight can't confirm. The timing is His, not ours. Every act of surrender creates space for supernatural supply. When God says go, He's already arranged what will meet you there. Provision may not come packaged in predictability, but it always arrives on purpose and always on time.

The Vision

Five years later, I can finally see what God was doing. What felt like leaving everything behind in South Carolina was really being positioned for expansion in Illinois. The obedience that once looked like loss has become the ground where God chose to enlarge our borders. The prayer of Jabez came alive in real time. He truly did "enlarge our coast," not by comfort but through calling.

When I look back, I see His fingerprints on every unseen detail. The home we left became a haven for another family. The help God showed me arrived for my family back home, just as He promised. My parents, both healed, now carry deeper testimonies of grace. My sons are thriving as young adults, learning, and shining in ways I once only prayed for. And me? I'm still building, still serving, still running my leg of the race with a greater understanding of what obedience really builds.

Isaiah 58:12 declares, *"And they that shall be of thee shall build the old waste places: thou shalt raise up the foundations of many generations ...*" That's what obedience does. It constructs something eternal. It lays down paths that others can dwell in. And Psalm 78:6-7 reminds us that the next generation might know and set their hope in God. That's the true weight of the baton—faith transferred, hope preserved, grace sustained.

Hebrews 12:1 tells us we are *"compassed about with so great a cloud of witnesses"* and calls us to *"run with patience the race that is set before us."* The generations behind us are watching. The generations ahead are waiting. And the weight we carry, when surrendered to God, becomes the strength they'll stand on.

Now, when I envision the race, I no longer see panic in the handoff. I see precision. I see faithfulness. Each runner gripping the baton, eyes fixed ahead, trusting that what's passed is holy and worth carrying.

The move didn't end a story; it expanded one. Every mile, every tear, every unseen yes became part of a larger testimony of God's faithfulness.

Obedience still enlarges territories.

Surrender still builds foundations.

And some stories of faithfulness are still being written.

Tawanda Ervin, PhD is Founder of ThriveWell Coaching and Consulting, LLC, where she shares motivational content for leaders navigating faith, family, and transition. A fourth-generation preacher and former pastor, she is a mother of three sons, including two on the autism spectrum. Passionate about encouraging neurodivergent families, Tawanda holds a Doctorate in Family, Marriage, and Children's Therapy and leadership coaching certifications.

3

GRACE TO GOVERN II

The Practitioners of Purpose

When Grace Trains the Hands That Build the Vision

Apostle Tiffany Bridges

Transformative leadership is never birthed in comfort—it is birthed in disruption. Grace, a blend of disruptive power, strategic wisdom, and divine generosity operating in human lives, teaches that disruption is not the end but the beginning of governance. Grace signals to us when it is time to move; our prophetic awareness and anointing allow us to perceive and prepare for change.

When leaders lead through grace, correction becomes restoration—not rejection. Teams flourish because grace creates cultures of trust rather than fear. Grace-governed leaders understand the rhythm of rotation. They don't cling to people or projects longer than Heaven does. They make room for succession, knowing every completed assignment births another.

Leader practitioners, Heaven's craftsmen, those who turn revelation into reform and grace into government, are called to apply revelation as working law in the earth. Their work is tested through the word, in the stewardship of their organizations. And for these leaders, disruption can be terrifying. Especially when we try to hold everything together by our own strength. But as believers, we know that disruption is not destruction—it's simply Heaven's construction crew moving in and preparing to tear stuff up to make room for something new.

Grace reveals that what is changing, what is collapsing around us or in us, is what no longer serves us. Grace builds courage in us to walk away from platforms that silence, relationships that diminish, and systems that exploit.

There comes a moment when a leader feels the quiet lifting of grace. The tools still work, and the words still flow, but the wind that once carried everything forward has shifted. That moment is sacred. It is Heaven's invitation to graduate.

I remember my grace-lifting moment clearly. I always served in various capacities of ministry. Opportunities to minister by song turned into an elevation to Worship Pastor. When I answered the call to rebuild a worship ministry and, eventually, with grace, helped them redefine and represent a changed charge and mission to our community, God's grace fell on that assignment.

In the beginning, everyone agreed on everything. It was wonderful, but slowly, little disagreements, pastor and board squabbles, began to emerge. As the fellowship began to feel the unrest among leadership, things took a turn. The harder we pushed to saturate the sanctuary with prayer, the more chaos and confusion snuck its way in.

One day, I went into the dark sanctuary to pray. In prayer, the Holy Spirit revealed to me that it was time to let go and move on. It had become hard for me to connect upward because I was distracted when I looked outward. Grace helped me to know it was time for me to move onto a new assignment in service of Him.

Once, I believed grace was simply the fuel that made completing assignments possible. I've learned that grace is the system that teaches us to manage what Heaven entrusts to us. Grace and its divine administration helps to fuel transitions from assignment to assignment. Grace is not solely emotional relief; it is divine administration. It constructs the unseen so we can steward the seen.

Grace healed me from the wounds of being overlooked, dismissed, and underestimated. But it did not stop there. Grace anointed me for a leadership I could not have claimed without it. Through grace, I became a builder of systems, a teacher of laws, and a practitioner of stewardship.

In my great mind, grace was a kind of holy eraser for failure, but then grace revealed itself as oil, sacred, fragrant, and multipurpose. Oil heals, yes. It soothes scars and covers cracks. But oil also consecrates. It marks someone for assignment, not just for comfort. Psalm 133:1-2 proclaims, *"Behold, how good and how pleasant it is for brethren to dwell together in unity! It is like the precious ointment upon the head, that ran down upon the beard, even Aaron's beard: that went down to the skirt of his garments."*

When God's grace oils your life, all protocols are suspended. God's goodness and mercy follow and speak for you. In His grace, you can let Him take full charge of all you do. Then, yokes are broken, and you get to enjoy the very best of God's provision.

When we speak of grace, we often picture the visionary—the dreamer with scrolls and Blueprints. What rarely gets discussed is disciplined execution; without grace, vision remains potential. Here, we practitioners—the ones who plan, implement, and manage purpose—are Heaven's project managers. We maintain the discipline that moves revelation into realization.

Grace trains the hands that build. It teaches rhythm, stillness, and release. Grace serves as a governor, helping us pace progress so obedience doesn't become exhaustion. It is the greatest leadership mentor of all time—teaching when to push, when to pause, and when to promote.

The Evolution of Grace

When grace exploded into my life in that dark sanctuary, this holy disruption, it didn't knock politely. It overturned my tables. Grace pulled me out of cycles of performance, rejection, and small thinking. It dared to show me that my worth wasn't tied to usefulness, and my future wasn't limited by evolving relationships.

Believe it or not, the anointing on your life evolves. Many of us are standing at a divine crossroads—the moment in every visionary's journey when what was once grace begins to feel like a grind. You're still showing up, still executing, but the wind that once pushed you forward has stilled, and now you must decide if it's time to change direction. For many, change blindsides us, and we perceive it as failure. That is not failure—it's transition. Every new dimension requires realignment; every charge requires release.

Ephesians 2:8-9 reassures us that grace is the currency Heaven issues when earth has run out of answers. *"For by grace are ye saved through faith; and that not of yourselves: it is the gift of God: Not of works, lest any man should boast."*

Here, grace is established as a zero-cost gift that saves—a spiritual currency that cannot be earned. The impact of grace on me has been transformational. It has left me no longer conformed to this world. Grace has walked me through fire without the smell of smoke, stretched my tent when I felt too small, and anointed my head with oil when my name was nearly erased.

Out of my own experiences in navigating grace and helping leaders grow came Bridges & Oil™—a mantle and a movement translating grace into leadership, programming, and community economy. We support leaders who are ready to activate their organizations and leadership teams in preparation for bold vision, new strategy, and enhanced stewardship.

We use organizational leadership principles to support leaders, teams, and entrepreneurs who have been called to do a work of God outside the four walls of the church. We support leaders as they develop parishioner engagement strategy and development rooted in Kingdom-based ideology.

Bridges and Oil™ is our testimony and a Blueprint for fellow practitioners called to impact communities not merely with intention but with the kind of thought leadership grace demands.

Some of my core revelations came each time grace stretched me—I learned that disruption is not destruction, experienced grace as oil that heals and anoints, and recognized Heaven's alerts that signal seasonal change.

That's why in Bridges & Oil™ programming, we begin with *The Mantle of Divine Disruption.* Stretching the Tent, or expanding our territory, isn't just about capacity; it's about courage. When practitioners allow grace to disrupt stale rhythms, they gain Blueprints for building beyond themselves.

Heaven's Alerts: Signs Your Season Is Closing

Grace is the bridge we walk while building it. Practitioners are often last to know when grace has shifted because we're wired to finish. We love structure, completion, and checking the box. Yet Heaven sends alerts that signal a new season before any door closes.

> Alert 1: Diminished Joy – You can still perform the task, but your spirit no longer sings in it. The fulfillment that once fueled you now feels forced.
>
> Alert 2: Unusual Resistance Without Revelation – Opposition without new instruction means grace is moving. There's a difference between warfare that refines and warfare that recycles.
>
> Alert 3: Absence of Fresh Instruction – Silence from Heaven invites new alignment. When innovation stops, review the assignment and release what's complete.

> Alert 4: Peace Lifts – You can still operate in skill, but you can't abide in stillness. The internal quiet that once covered you now feels distant.

When peace departs, it's not punishment—it's propulsion. Heaven uses discomfort as direction. Grace doesn't only anoint what you do; it reroutes and recalibrates.

Recalibration follows release: Quiet yourself to hear new instruction. In stillness, revisit boundaries, pace, and priorities. Let God become the technician. Heaven resets your leadership settings so you can hear clearly again.

As Maya Angelou once said, "And still like dust I rise." Rising into new assignments with humility and fresh oil allows you to reenter your path on purpose and without residue. Yesterday's experience is meant to inform you not imprison you.

Grace graduates us when we've mastered stewardship at one level. With every pivot comes promotion in disguise. Grace will never demote you; it delegates new dimensions of trust.

To leaders who manage people and purpose, grace is your most important HR policy. It teaches you how to handle those who've outgrown assignments, just as God once handled you. When grace lifts from a team member, performance may remain, but presence fades. The temptation is to control; grace invites you to coach.

To every builder, manager, and steward reading these words—you are Heaven's hands on earth. Visionaries may dream, but you ensure dreams become systems. You are anchors and stabilizers of destiny. Grace isn't finished with you; it's inviting you to mature. It's calling you from management's mechanics into the miracle of partnership.

Letting go is never a loss—it's Heaven's math of multiplying capacity, one obedient release at a time.

When peace departs, don't panic. Heaven is simply shifting your desk. Release what's complete, recalibrate your pace, and rise into your next assignment. Grace will be waiting to meet you, whispering, "Welcome to your next level of governance."

Leadership by Grace

Leadership by grace asks three questions before every decision:

1. Is this person's season complete or simply challenged?
2. Am I protecting comfort or nurturing calling?
3. Is this transition about release or reinforcement?

Attribution Note

Scripture quotations are from the King James Version (public domain). Quotation from Maya Angelou's "Still I Rise" is used with proper attribution for educational and inspirational purposes.

Originality Statement

I, Apostle Tiffany Bridges, affirm that this work titled *Grace to Govern II: The Practitioners of Purpose* is an original composition written solely by me. Except for the clearly attributed Scripture passages and brief quotation from Maya Angelou's "Still I Rise," all language, structure, and conceptual framing—including the metaphors, phrases, and teachings—are original expressions of my lived revelation and authorship. This manuscript has not been copied, republished, or adapted from any other author, work, or source, and it remains the exclusive intellectual and creative property of the author.

Apostle Tiffany Bridges of the Orlando, Florida area is a prophetic strategist and founder of Bridges & Oil™, equipping leaders to steward Heaven's blueprints with grace and authority. Entering her Jubilee year, she champions divine reset, restoration, and governed expansion. Her work activates practitioners to rise in purpose and power. **Connect with Apostle Tiffany at BridgesAndOil.com.**

4

FROM THE HEART OF A FIRSTBORN

Morris J. Crawford

I want to describe my life: what I've lived, learned, and tried to pass to the next generation. I accepted Christ at twelve and sensed something different about myself. I didn't anger easily and often let things go. Growing up as the oldest of eight and the pastor's firstborn son, I was corrected often and learned hard lessons under a firm hand. Over time, prayer became my refuge, and from my heart, I discovered that God answers sincere prayers. These stories are my proof.

> *"Call unto me, and I will answer thee, and show thee great and mighty things ..."* (Jeremiah 33:3).

The Nickel and the Soldering Iron (Butchy)

Our neighbor Butchy was my age. He discovered my mother gave me a nickel each day for milk and threatened me with red-hot soldering irons: "Give me your nickel or I'll burn your eyes." Terrified, I gave him my nickel daily for weeks. I told no one. I only prayed, "Lord, please do something."

One day, Butchy disappeared from school. When his mother asked us to visit, I found him in a full body cast—injured after being hit by a truck. I was shocked and fearful but also relieved. He never asked me for money again, and we became friends. I learned God sees the fears we can't say out loud, and He knows how to deliver.

Lesson & Legacy: Tell God the truth when you can't tell anyone else; He can change what you can't control.

> *"I sought the LORD, and he heard me, and delivered me from all my fears"* (Psalm 34:4).

Melrose and the Beehive

In Salisbury, NC, my neighbor Melrose and I found a beehive inside a bush. Mischief got the best of me, so I dared her to squeeze the hive and offered her a nickel. She did it—and the bees swarmed, stinging her badly. I lied to cover myself. Two years later in church, a hornet nailed the back of my shaved head. I rolled on the floor in pain until an elder drew out the stinger. All I could think of was Melrose crying like I once made her cry.

Lesson & Legacy: Sin sown in secret returns in public. Repent early; repent fully.

> *"Be not deceived; God is not mocked: for whatsoever a man soweth, that shall he also reap"* (Galatians 6:7).
>
> *"He that covereth his sins shall not prosper: but whoso confesseth and forsaketh them shall have mercy"* (Proverbs 28:13).

The Newspaper Prize and the Glutton's Photo

In Detroit, I won a circulation contest, and the prize was a trip to Frankenmuth. The meal was "all you can eat," so I did—chicken, sides, bread, dessert—until I couldn't move. A photographer staged a picture of me "about to eat a whole chicken." Two weeks later, the photo hit the city paper: "We told him he could eat all he wanted—and he did." My pastor-father saw it, preached on gluttony, and disciplined me.

Lesson & Legacy: Appetite without restraint becomes shame. Thank God for loving discipline.

> *"Be not among winebibbers; among riotous eaters of flesh: For the drunkard and the glutton shall come to poverty …"* (Proverbs 23:20-21).
>
> *"For whom the Lord loveth he chasteneth …"* (Hebrews 12:6).

"Ain't No Colored Santa Claus"

At school in North Carolina, the Santa who entered the cafeteria was a Black man with a cotton beard. I'd never seen that and started yelling, "Ain't no colored Santa Claus!" I ran, grabbed salt, threw it, and hit Santa in the eyes. My father carried me out with a belt on my backside. Years later in Detroit, I woke to help Dad unload boxes onto our car. I realized: my father had been my "Santa" all along.

Lesson & Legacy: Immaturity mocks what it doesn't understand; truth humbles and matures us. Honor those who quietly provide.

> *"Buy the truth, and sell it not; also wisdom, and instruction, and understanding"* (Proverbs 23:23).
>
> *"And ye shall know the truth, and the truth shall make you free"* (John 8:32).

Jesus Burning in My Furnace

In Chicago with six children and an oil furnace on empty (two 250-gallon drums below "E"), I still set the thermostat at 90 by faith and went job-hunting. For nearly two weeks, the furnace kept running. Each night, I checked the gauge—still below empty. The day I received my first paycheck and headed to buy oil, the furnace finally turned off. God had carried us.

Lesson & Legacy: When you put your family in God's hands, He puts His provision in your house.

> *"I have been young, and now am old; yet have I not seen the righteous forsaken, nor his seed begging bread"* (Psalm 37:25).

> *"... my God shall supply all your need according to his riches in glory by Christ Jesus"* (Philippians 4:19).

220 Volts of Mercy

While installing infrared heaters 30 feet up, a live 220-volt line stuck my hand to the unit. I couldn't let go. I shouted the only Name I had: "Jesus!" Suddenly, I fell between the scaffolds onto a plank—alive, shaken, grateful. I call it my *electrifying testimony.*

Lesson & Legacy: When you can't release what's killing you, call on the Name that can release you.

> *"When thou passest through the waters, I will be with thee ... when thou walkest through the fire, thou shalt not be burned ..."* (Isaiah 43:2).

> *"... the name of Jesus Christ of Nazareth ..."* (Acts 3:6).

Gold Coins and "All A's"

I carry shiny gold coins to inspire students. I ask: "Have you ever held real gold?" Most say no. I put a coin in their hand and tell them: "Work for all A's—scholarships find excellence." Then, I give them my riddle: "If I gave you an A for every A you earned, how many A's would you get?" Most answer with numbers. I say, "It's a three-letter word—all." Aim for your best, not just "enough."

Lesson & Legacy: Excellence glorifies God and opens doors.

"As for these four children, God gave them knowledge and skill . . ." (Daniel 1:17).

"And whatsoever ye do, do it heartily, as to the Lord . . ." (Colossians 3:23).

Fatherly Counsel for a New Generation

Pray first. God hears heart-truths you can't tell others (Jeremiah 33:3).

Tell the truth. Confession prevents harvests you don't want (Proverbs 28:13; Galatians 6:7).

Control appetite. Discipline today prevents shame tomorrow (Proverbs 23:20-21).

Honor providers. Many blessings come through quiet hands (Proverbs 23:23).

Trust God's provision. He keeps homes warm and hearts steady (Psalm 37:25; Philippians 4:19).

Call on Jesus. In danger, His Name delivers (Isaiah 43:2; Acts 3:6).

Pursue excellence. Aim for "all A's" in character, not just grades (Colossians 3:23; Daniel 1:17).

Impacting a Generation

My stories are simple, but the God behind them is not. If we train our children to pray first, tell the truth, honor discipline, and pursue excellence, they will meet the God who answers by fire and by furnace heat set on "empty." Let parents, pastors, teachers, and neighbors govern with grace so our kids can grow with courage.

> *"Train up a child in the way he should go: and when he is old, he will not depart from it"* (Proverbs 22:6).

May these short stories become long roots in the next generation—so they rise as truthful, grateful, excellent sons and daughters who carry the Brand of Christ with honor.

Minister Morris J. Crawford, Sr., eldest son of a pastor, was raised in Detroit with strong Christian values and a relentless work ethic. A Master Carpenter Builder, he helped construct major Chicago skyscrapers, taught building trades at Olive Harvey College, and later owned Hammer-Time Construction. A proud father of ten, including Dr. Deborah C. Anthony, he now ministers at The Restoration House in Gary, Indiana, sharing testimonies that restore hope and help men rebuild their lives on the foundation of Christ.

SECTION II: REMEMBRANCE & TRUTH

5

GRACED TO PRESERVE

Earlye Julien, M.S., Ed.

Key Scripture: Exodus 16:32

Just as the meeting with my supervisor was about to start, the phone rang. I actually welcomed the interruption, as I could feel my stomach fluttering from the uneasiness of the conversation that was about to take place. When the phone call ended, he turned toward me and assumed a thinker's pose, which I had witnessed numerous times before. He leaned back slightly in his chair with his hands behind his head, interlocking his fingers. Though his posture was visually relaxed, I knew he was mentally engaged in active thought. He rattled off several options, with each resulting in the same dead end.

Finally, he leaned forward, instantly conveying that all options had been exhausted, and stated, "Well, we know you can handle implementing processes well, but can you handle the tough stuff?" He was referring to an employee he had already discerned months prior would result in an involuntary termination, and I would be responsible to execute that task. Initially, my stomach was tied in knots just thinking about the inevitable event. While it was one of the toughest things I've ever had to do, I had been equipped for such a time as this. Not only had my supervisor mentored me throughout the years, but I was equally blessed to have parents and grandparents who had modeled and taught me the Christian principles necessary to handle the tough things in life.

We are reminded in John 16:33 of the following:

> *"... In the world ye shall have tribulation: but be of good cheer; I have overcome the world."*

Whether leading as a parent, supervisor, teacher, corporate executive, military leader, government official, ministry team leader, coach, project leader, pastor, or entrepreneur, or in another leadership role, there will come a time when besides overseeing an operation or function itself, you will have to handle some "tough stuff."

My parents wanted better for my life than what they had experienced. Likewise, it has been my heart's desire to position my children for greater success than my own. I didn't want them to experience some of the struggles and tribulations I had endured. In fact, I did my best to protect them. Yet as I faced this tough situation with total confidence in God, I was uncertain whether I had effectively passed on to my children the triumphant testimonies that had cultivated such hope.

I gleaned from the wealth of experiential wisdom, practical knowledge, Biblical teaching, and powerful testimonies of God's faithfulness that had been preserved by my grandparents and parents and passed down to me. I couldn't help but wonder whether my children were ill-prepared. Had I shielded them too much? Had I failed to see the glory in my children's tribulations? Had I unintentionally impeded opportunities for character growth and faith development that were necessary to withstand trouble? I was reminded of what the Bible teaches us about tribulations:

> "*… we have access by faith into this grace wherein we stand, and rejoice in hope of the glory of God. And not only so, but we glory in tribulations also: knowing that tribulation worketh patience; And patience, experience; and experience, hope*" (Romans 5:2-4).

This legacy of confident faith, inherited from prior generations, allows us to withstand and even grow from tough times because we've learned to lean and depend on God and operate in the power of the Holy Spirit.

As young adults, my children now feel fairly comfortable talking with my husband and me about the troubles they face. They have often said to us, "You guys made adulting look easy. We didn't expect it to be so hard!" While our desire as parents may be to shield our children from trouble, the truth is, there will be trouble. While we should make every effort to keep them safe, we can never totally shield them from trouble. Rather, we must teach them how to depend on the God of Angel Armies who can and will bring them through it. Just as Moses reminded the new generation of Israelites to remember God's triumphs over their trouble, parents must remind their children as well. Once God brings our children through trouble, they must never, ever forget that any good thing they have inherited or success they may have achieved is not by their own might but of the Lord's, and they, in turn, must remind their children of the same.

> "*... when the Lord thy God shall have brought thee into the land which he sware unto thy fathers, to Abraham, to Isaac, and to Jacob, to give thee great and goodly cities, which thou buildest not, And houses full of all good things, which thou filledst not, and wells digged, which thou diggedst not, vineyards and olive trees, which thou plantedst not; when thou shalt have eaten and be full; Then beware lest thou forget the Lord, which brought thee forth out of the land of Egypt, from the house of bondage*" (Deuteronomy 6:10-15).

God delivered the children of Israel from the bondage of slavery in Egypt with numerous miracles. Yet about a month after their exit, they had already forgotten what God had done. They were wandering in the wilderness and complained that they had no food. Moses and Aaron told the people that by evening they would know that the Lord had brought them out of Egypt, and in the morning, they would see the glory of the Lord. God performed yet another miracle. He caused quail to come to the camp in the evenings and rained down bread from Heaven in the mornings to sustain them.

It was here in Exodus 16:32 that I received a strategy to impact generations, beginning with my own children:

> *"And Moses said, This is the thing which the Lord commandeth, Fill an omer of it to be kept for your generations; that they may see the bread wherewith I have fed you in the wilderness, when I brought you forth from the land of Egypt."*

That container of manna was to be preserved. It was to be guarded, watched over, and protected as a valuable reminder and testimony for future generations to see evidence of how God provided and to make sure His mighty works would never be forgotten.

Likewise, we have a rich heritage that must be preserved. The Word of God, our Identity in Him, and our beliefs, practices, stories, and testimonies of the great things God has done must be guarded, watched over, and protected with efforts equivalent to those we would employ to preserve expensive possessions for our children's future inheritance.

Below are three methods the Bible recommends for effective preservation:

1. You can preserve by practicing. Children learn by watching and mimicking. As we live out our faith before them and put the glory of God on display, our children will adopt our way of life as their own.

> *"Those thing, which ye have both learned, and received, and heard, and seen in me, do: and the God of peace shall be with you"* (Philippians 4:9).

2. You can preserve by intentionally teaching your children. Each generation has a responsibility to teach the next generation. Psalm 78:5-8 states:

   > *"For he established a testimony in Jacob, and appointed a law in Israel, which he commanded our fathers, that they should make them known to their children: That the generation to come might know them, even the children which should be born; who should arise and declare them to their children: That they might set their hope in God, and not forget the works of God, but keep his commandments: And might not be as their fathers, a stubborn and rebellious generation; a generation that set not their heart aright, and whose spirit was not stedfast with God."*

   We teach the next generation so they will know God, so they will trust God, so they will obey His commands, and so they won't become a stubborn and rebellious generation.

3. Finally, you can preserve by sharing your personal stories and testimonies.

   As I started working on this writing project, it felt as though I had been suddenly catapulted into a season of trouble. I experienced a death in the family, the death of a close friend, numerous stressful situations at work, some financial challenges, a backlog of things to do at home and in the ministry, and some annoying health issues. I was still determined to finish what I had started, so I kept plugging away. Just as I started to see a light at the end of the tunnel, I was hit with another unexpected curveball. A routine checkup revealed abnormal tissue that caused my doctor concern. So, I was referred to a specialist for a biopsy. Unfortunately, I wouldn't get the results for two whole weeks. That was pretty much all I could bear.

I started preparing a letter to Dr. Anthony, the visionary and founding author for *Graced to Govern – Impacting a Generation (Series 2).* I wanted to thank her for the opportunity and let her know that due to the trouble in my life right now, I wouldn't be able to proceed. I started looking through my email to find one from her that was addressed to me so I could just hit reply and start writing my withdrawal email. I found one but didn't read the content because I was just trying to reply. Somehow, I accidentally clicked on a link within the email. Unbeknownst to me, it was the recording of the last meeting she had conducted with the other authors. I had absolutely no intention of watching the recording. Afterall, I was withdrawing from the project, so it would be of no benefit to me. Plus, I thought it might be a little depressing to watch the rest of the cohort expressing their progress, when mine had come to a screeching halt. Nevertheless, I was warring within myself. There was an undeniable force drawing me—a still, small voice saying, "Watch the video." Little did I know, my feelings of hopelessness were about to be arrested.

After a few hellos and a powerful opening prayer, Dr. Anthony announced a slight change in her typical meeting agenda. Before moving forward with the meeting, she was going to allow someone to share a testimony. She announced Dr. Latricia Williams, and shortly thereafter, a beautiful woman appeared on the screen. The compassion and conviction with which she started her testimony immediately commanded my attention. She explained how just the week before, she had discovered a lump in her breast. Her doctor confirmed her finding and sent her to a specialist for a biopsy. At that moment, I realized that her story was my story. I was speechless! How could this be? Who set this up? Within minutes, she exploded with thanksgiving about the glorious deeds God had done. The lump that was there last week couldn't be found! I couldn't stop crying because Dr. Williams' testimony reminded me about my own past testimonies and the testimonies of my parents and grandparents. Like the children of Israel, I had allowed myself to focus on the trouble and needed to be reminded of all the miracles I've seen and all the stories I've heard that have been passed down to my generation. Because Dr. Williams was willing to be transparent and share her story about what God had done for her, I was reminded of the character of God, His power, and His might. My hopelessness turned to expectant hope, all because she told her story.

> *"Give ear, O my people, to my law: incline your ears to the words of my mouth. I will open my mouth in a parable: I will utter dark sayings of old: Which we have heard and known, and our fathers have told us. We will not hide them from their children, shewing to the generation to come the praises of the Lord, and his strength, and his wonderful works that he hath done"* (Psalm 78:1-4).

Praise God, I received a good report! The abnormal tissue that caused my doctor concern was benign. God has blessed me with another testimony to preserve and pass down to the next generation to give them hope in times of tribulation. Likewise, the stories and testimonies of how God has helped you overcome the troubles you've faced is extremely valuable. It's your responsibility to guard them, watch over them, and protect them so they can be passed on for the success of future generations. You're graced to preserve!

Earlye's passion is writing to encourage and uplift the Body of Christ. She serves in ministry alongside her husband Pastor Angelo (A.J.) Julien, campus pastor of River City Church, Uptown Campus in Moline, IL and is a proud mother to their two gifted sons, Wesley and Jacobe. She has earned Master's degrees in Counseling and Educational Administration and supports life-long learning.

You can find her at: https://www.facebook.com/earlye.julien

6

IMPACTING A GENERATION THROUGH TRUTH

Pastors Tracy and Dena Lowery

"I have no greater joy than to hear that my children walk in truth." 3 John 1:4

The world we live in today is much different from the one we remember as adolescents. Although it was by no means a perfect world, we somewhat knew what to expect day to day. Now, we encounter a society filled with individuals who live in fear and anxiety with no hope for their future. The news and social media are overflowing with reports of murders, missing persons, warfare, and traumatic events. The division of races, confusion of identities, and disagreements in political stances has caused discord even amongst those who call themselves the body of Christ. Where can future leaders and our next generation turn to build a foundational structure in their lives that will not crumble under the pressure of all this chaos? The answer is found in 3 John 1:4: "*I have no greater joy than to hear that my children walk in truth.*"

As we read this scripture, it resonated deeply within us. We acknowledge that John was referring to his children that had been birthed in the family of God when he said, "my children." As parents and pastors, our biological and spiritual children are our most valuable gifts from the Lord, other than salvation. We understand that John was revealing to us the fundamental necessity of walking in the truth, especially for those we are responsible for and mentor. It is a core principle for the well-being and survival of those we love so dearly.

Truth in a Confused Generation

We both were brought up in Christian homes that instilled in us to walk in truth. If God said it, we just believed it. We were taught that the Word of God is truth. In John 17:17, it states "*Sanctify them through thy truth: thy word is truth.*" There was no room for questioning God's Word or His voice. If a man or woman of God gave instructions from the Lord, we obeyed. We were taught that if they were wrong, then God would still honor our obedience, and every false prophet would be revealed. Our confidence was in God, whom we reverenced and feared, and not the human being. God and His Word had permanence in our homes and lives.

Over the years, it seems as if the truth gradually stopped being taught. This belief system and lifestyle of walking in truth is now viewed as harsh and restrictive, lacking all the joys of freedom of choice. Human ideologies, scientific discoveries, even experiences and opinions of influential persons have taken the place of God's Word. You can choose to believe whomever or whatever you desire, and that will be your "truth." The result is we now have a world filled with "*blind leaders of the blind*" (Matthew 15:14).

Clarifying Misconceptions

Let's clarify some misunderstandings of the truth. God's Word is not restrictive or cruel. It will not put you in a prison void of all joys; that is a lie of the enemy. The truth does not imprison you; it protects you and affirms you with the right to live free. "*If the Son therefore shall make you free, ye shall be free indeed*" (John 8:36).

1. The truth will set you free - free from depression, free from fears and anxieties, free to taste the goodness of God.

> "*And ye shall know the truth, and the truth shall make you free*" (John 8:32).
>
> "*To appoint unto them that mourn in Zion, to give unto them beauty for ashes, the oil of joy for mourning, the garment of praise for the spirit of heaviness; that they might be called trees of righteousness, the planting of the Lord, that he might be glorified*" (Isaiah 61:3).

2. The Word of God brings hope, joy, and peace, and it comforts brokenness.

   "Now the God of hope fill you with all joy and peace in believing, that ye may abound in hope, through the power of the Holy Ghost" (Romans 15:13).

   "The Lord is nigh unto them that are of a broken heart; and saveth such as be of a contrite spirit" (Psalm 34:18).

3. The truth also is filled with promises of protection.

   "The Lord shall preserve thee from all evil: he shall preserve thy soul. The Lord shall preserve thy going out and thy coming in from this time forth, and even for evermore" (Psalm 121:7-8).

   "Every word of God is pure: he is a shield unto them that put their trust in him" (Proverbs 30:5).

The Deviated Path

The world is lacking the ability to walk in the truth because either there has been a rejection of the Word of God, or past leaders have failed to teach it. This is why the world today is overwhelmed with so much hopelessness and confusion. Neglecting to seek God and to search the scriptures in every situation is comparable to an unarmed soldier showing up for battle.

As parents, we place so much of our time, effort, and resources to ensure our children will have a successful life and to secure their futures. We place them in sports and other extracurricular activities so they will be well-rounded, healthy individuals. We encourage them to study, ensure they are properly educated, and put money aside for college expenses. We may even purchase properties or life insurance policies or invest in stocks so that we can leave an inheritance. Although all these things are commendable, the most precious contribution we could bestow upon our children is to arm them with the truth and how to walk in it.

The Truth Is the Cure

God warned us in His Word, *"For the time will come when they will not endure sound doctrine; but after their own lusts shall they heap to themselves teachers, have itching ears"* (2 Timothy 4:3). As leaders, our love and compassion require that we provide our people with what they need to survive and thrive, even if it means denying them what they desire when it is contrary to the truth. We are not called to soothe the itch when we hold the cure for the condition. There is a difference between relief and healing. There is also a significant difference between relief and freedom. David played his harp and brought Saul relief. We are not raising Sauls; we are training Davids. Therefore, we must provide them with ALL of the truth. *"All scripture is given by inspiration of God, and is profitable for doctrine, for reproof, for correction, for instruction in righteousness: That the man of God may be perfect, thoroughly furnished unto all good works"* (2 Timothy 3:16-17).

Declaration and Proclamation

We declare and proclaim that a generation is emerging, one that will walk in truth with a boldness and strength unlike any before it. They are structured, equipped, and prepared to withstand any battle they may encounter. Because they have found their Identity in Christ, they are empowered with lasting inner peace and true belonging. They trust and rely upon every word of God and therefore are established as a unified generation of the Lord, one that stands firm against fleeting trends and beyond the reach of deception.

Mandate That Will Leave a Legacy

Those who have been graced by God to hold leadership positions have the ability to bring change upon the Earth.

> *We will not hide them from their children, shewing to the generation to come the praises of the Lord, and his strength, and his wonderful works that he hath done. For he established a testimony in Jacob, and appointed a law in Israel, which he commanded our fathers, that they should make them known to their children: That the generation to come might know them, even the children which should be born; who should arise and declare them to their children: That they might set their hope in God, and not forget the works of God, but keep his commandments"* (Psalm 78:4-7).

This is a mandate, not a mere invitation, for leaders to lay a foundational structure of truth for all future generations. In embracing this mandate, our children will put their confidence in God, do as He commands, and ensure their children and their grandchildren know His ways.

Pastors Tracy and **Dena Lowery** *faithfully serve as lead pastors of The Saviour's House in Fayetteville, North Carolina, continuing the legacy of Dena's mother, Pastor Sylvia Keller. With over 20 years of ministry, they have witnessed countless miracles and transformed lives. Blessed with three children, their desire is to see souls saved, healed, and delivered by the power of Jesus Christ.*

7

IF YOU FEED THEM, THEY WILL COME!

Dr. Alice Maria Crawford

It's been many years ago now, but there was a time in life when I noticed my family dynamics were changing. Five of my eight biological children had grown up to the point that they were no longer living in my house. Number six was straining at the bit and doing everything he could to leave. Only the oldest two girls were married. As for the rest of them, I was concerned as to what kind of choices they would make in their newfound freedom as adults.

I remembered the days when we all were under one roof. There were challenges to be sure. Yet, as I reflected on the good memories, so many had to do with Sunday dinners, birthday and graduation celebrations, often with extended family. Summer days spent going to the beach, museums and parks; and many, many days breaking bread with family at church. The thought formulated in my mind that most of our better days were with all of us together around a table sharing our meals.

My only concern was not for what path my children were trying to forge, wondering whether their choices would keep them in the faith. I also considered how to keep them together as a family. I had witnessed so many families grow apart as the children branched out on their own. I did not want this to be our experience.

One day I heard the words – *"if you feed them, they will come"*. What did that mean? Seeking the Lord for an answer, He reminded me that no matter how many problems we would have during the week; after church on Sunday, when I would make Sunday dinner, this was always a bright spot of the week. As I thought on this, I realized that this was something I could easily do; prepare Sunday dinner and invite everyone over. This soon became a ritual. I discovered that even as adults they were willing to pass up their favorite restaurants for a home-cooked meal!

Now the next question was, what would the agenda be? I knew the guys would easily slip into watching whatever game was on the television, but this would not promote real family time. So, again the Lord spoke and said to use this forum to celebrate milestones. With eight children, two nephews, their spouses and significant others – there was always someone that had a birthday, or other accomplishment to recognize. If it was a birthday, we would go around the room and issue that person a birthday blessing on their special day. This would lead to sharing memories and extending encouragement to the person being celebrated. This soon became a time that everyone looked forward to, after all who doesn't like to be celebrated!

From my daily Bible reading I noticed that God encouraged celebrations! From the Lord directing the children of Israel to set aside times of celebration, such as in Deuteronomy 16:15, and Leviticus 23:41, throughout the Old Testament as in Ecclesiastes 3:12-15, or Nehemiah 8:10. It did not stop in the New Testament, however. Jesus' first miracle was of turning water into wine at a wedding (John 2:1-11)! Revelation 19:9 shows us that all believers will celebrate at the marriage supper of the lamb. Reading of the many celebrations in the Bible, encouraged me to know that God delights in His people coming together to recognize significant events.

As time went on, I saw the family really coming together again. What began to evolve from celebrating special days, became times of family prayer. For many years, once a month we had family prayer. Those were times we began to see the mighty hand of God at work in each of our lives. When it seemed impossible for promotions on their jobs, after prayer, they came into fruition. Even when there were challenges on jobs, after prayer we always saw how God worked in the favor of the one challenged. Many sicknesses were healed. God was very active in our lives and one by one, each of the children placed their faith in the God they grew up hearing about. He was no longer just the God of their pastor grandfather, or that of their praying grandmother, He became their God. I am blessed to say that five pastors have emerged from within this group, and all my children have vocations that honorably serve their communities. Another worthy benefit that evolved has been, that as they married and had children of their own, they began to incorporate family prayer in their own homes!

Over the years, the word spread to extended family and friends, of what God was doing in family prayer. Others would join us and eventually the prayer time took on an annual set time for corporate prayer. Life brought about changes and several of my children and extended family moved out of the local area making it impossible for all to meet in person. God who knows the end from the beginning, knew that it would not be long before we would all be in the same room again. The introduction of facetime came about, and later Zoom. Though separated by distance and time zones, we could once again be together to rejoice in our GOD and lifting each other's needs. To this day we continue having regular family prayer on Zoom.

Just the other day, I got a text from one of my daughter's best friends thanking me for introducing family prayer. She told me that she followed the practice of bringing her family together for dinner and family prayer and they have been blessed to see radical changes in their family.

Of course, every family is different. How you bring your family together may take on a different form. Even though we began with Sunday dinner, any occasion can be celebrated, even if it is just celebrating the gift of life! However, if household salvation is you goal, then Jesus must be made the center, and not the celebration itself. I believe just as He led our family step by step, He has a plan for all families to do as He admonished the children of Israel so long ago:

> 6-7 *Write these commandments that I've given you today on your hearts. Get them inside of you and then get them inside your children. Talk about them wherever you are, sitting at home or walking in the street; talk about them from the time you get up in the morning to when you fall into bed at night...*
>
> 25 *"It will be a set-right and put-together life for us if we make sure that we do this entire commandment in the Presence of God, our God, just as he commanded us to do." Deuteronomy 6:6-7:25 (Message)*

Dr. Crawford worked with youth and young adults in her profession as a teacher, and in church as a youth leader. As a mother, the most important gift she thought to give her own eight children was to teach what it means to be a Christian.

She founded HeartLife Ministries to provide a forum for young leaders to have opportunity to utilize their gifts. Writing Bible-based messages on Christian living has been her focus over the years.

Continuing to invest in the spiritual formation of the next generation, she gives as much love and support as she can to her twenty-nine grandchildren and eight great grandchildren. God has also afforded her the privilege of doing weekly Bible studies. Her hope is to continue to upbuild the Kingdom of God as she has opportunity.

8

THE POWER OF A MULTI-GENERATIONAL FAMILY ENDURING THE PROCESS

Maria Bristol-Reed

Introduction: A Time of Connection Rooted in God's Design

In our house, Sunday dinners were more than food; they were sacred. My hands moved with purpose as I cooked recipes passed down through generations while Mama shared stories—some true, some touched with her special kind of wisdom—and my grandbabies asked the kind of wild, beautiful questions only a child could think of. Four generations gathered at one table, each in a different season of life, yet all held together by faith, love, and growth.

These dinners reflected God's design for family. As Genesis 1:28 says, *"Be fruitful, and multiply, and replenish the earth"* not only through children but through legacy, stewardship, and spiritual multiplication. We are more than relatives; we are a living ecosystem of memory, strength, and grace. Though imperfect, we are bound together by the One who is perfect. With God as the head of our family, we are learning to love deeply, walk in truth, honor one another, and stand in integrity because that is what truly holds us together.

God's Design for Multi-Generational Families: A Biblical Perspective

God's design for family, especially in multi-generational households, emphasizes connection, support, and shared values across generations. Grandparents pass down wisdom, life lessons, and cultural heritage, providing stability and perspective, while younger members bring energy and fresh ideas. Together, they create a balanced, enriching environment. Families support one another through challenges, fostering unity, resilience, and love. Each member plays a vital role in sustaining traditions, nurturing faith, and building a sense of Identity and belonging. In this way, multi-generational families reflect God's original design of teaching and learning, spiritual growth, mutual care, and community building, shaping not only their own households but the generations and communities to come.

"We will not hide them from their children, shewing to the generation to come the praises of the Lord, and his strength, and his wonderful works that he hath done. For he established a testimony in Jacob, and appointed a law in Israel, which he commanded our fathers, that they should make them known to their children: That the generation to come might know them, even the children which should be born; who should arise and declare them to their children" (Psalm 78:4-6).

> *"Children's children are the crown of old men; and the glory of children are their fathers"* (Proverbs 17:6).

The Bible reinforces the idea that families are meant to nurture, support, and uplift one another, passing down faith and values through the generations.

Enduring the Journey: From Turmoil to Joy

When my baby brother passed, the grief that hit our family was like nothing I'd ever felt. It wasn't just sadness; it was like the whole world had shifted. Time didn't move the same. The silence that followed wasn't peaceful; it was heavy. It echoed with everything we had lost and everything that would never be.

My mama carried the deepest pain. You could see it in her eyes, even when she didn't say a word. But somehow, she kept going. Her strength wasn't loud; it was quiet and steady. She moved through each day with grace, holding a pain that could've broken her, but choosing to stay present for the rest of us. She'd been through storms before, but this one was different. And still, she stood.

She didn't talk much about her grief, but her actions said everything. We cried together when we needed to, and we prayed when words wouldn't come. And through it all, God's presence held us down. That scripture in Psalm 34:18 came alive for me: *"The Lord is nigh unto them that are of a broken heart; and saveth such as be of a contrite spirit."*

Watching my mama walk through that kind of loss taught me something deep. Strength isn't about not feeling pain; it's about choosing to keep going anyway. Our love didn't fix everything, but it kept us together. And slowly, joy started to creep back in. Not loud, but soft. In shared laughter, in honoring memories, in the quiet strength of a woman who refused to let grief have the final say.

Even the grandkids, who usually kept to themselves, showed up in their own way. They didn't ask questions or try to fix anything. They just stayed close, sharing a snack, sitting in silence, listening to the wind. That's the beauty of family across generations. It teaches without preaching. It heals without pressure. It loves without conditions.

The Process: Life's Shared Journey

Going through life's ups and downs—that's the real journey. It's not just about the good times or the hard hits; it's about how we grow through it all. Whether it's money struggles, health scares, losing someone you love, or celebrating new life and love at weddings and births, having a family that spans generations makes all the difference.

Emotional strength: Grandma and Grandpa bring that old-school wisdom; our parents guide us with what they've learned; and the kids? They remind us what hope looks like.

Teamwork: We share the load. When one of us is tired, someone else steps in. That kind of support keeps you from feeling alone.

Keeping the legacy alive: The way we talk, the values we hold, the traditions we pass down—they don't just survive; they thrive because we keep them going together.

In a multi-generational family, you don't walk through life alone. You walk with people who've been where you're going and who love you enough to walk beside you no matter what.

Wisdom That Walks Beside You; Traditions That Ground You

In our family, wisdom doesn't come in fancy speeches; it lives in the way we show up for one another, in the stories we tell, and in the traditions we refuse to let go. Like Proverbs 4:7 says, "*Wisdom is the principal thing; therefore get wisdom: and with all thy getting get understanding.*" My mama once told me, "You don't have to be strong all the time. You just have to keep showing up." I didn't know what that meant until life knocked me down. But those words became my anchor, lining up perfectly with Galatians 6:9, reminding me not to grow weary because in due time, faithfulness brings a harvest.

Living in a multi-generational home has shown me that wisdom is not just taught—it is lived. It shows up in how we love, how we endure, and how we lift one another up, just like Ecclesiastes 4:9-10 teaches us: We rise together. And that same wisdom is embedded in our family traditions, especially the way we gather. Birthdays aren't just about cake; they are sacred markers of God's faithfulness. Every prayer my mother prays over us, every laugh from the children, every plate passed around the table—it all speaks. It reminds us of how far God has brought us and how His love holds us together.

My daddy's wisdom shaped me too. He taught me that our choices have power and that complaining without action is surrendering our authority. In the same way, our family traditions teach our children who they are and whose they are. When we gather, pray, celebrate, and forgive, we are passing down more than memories; we are passing down governance. We are teaching the next generation how to lead homes, churches, and communities with grace, strength, and accountability.

Because in our house, wisdom walks with us and tradition roots us. Together they form the roadmap of faith that ensures our children will not just survive this world but lead it with unwavering conviction and Godly purpose.

Conflict and Healing Across Generations

Our family has had its share of tension. One moment that sticks with me happened after my grandmother passed. Amid grief, a misunderstanding with a cousin created distance between us. Instead of speaking, we let silence settle in.

Healing didn't come through confrontation but through time and my mama's gentle words: "You don't need to justify yourself to be understood. Just be willing to love despite the misunderstanding." Her wisdom didn't erase the hurt, but it cracked the door open. Eventually, my cousin and I talked, not to rehash but to remember our bond. That conversation softened the space between us.

In multi-generational families like ours, grace runs deep. Conflict is part of life, but so is forgiveness. Sometimes, reconciliation comes through humility, shared memories, or simply saying, "I miss you." When love is the foundation, healing is always possible. As Ephesians 4:32 reminds us, *"And be ye kind to one another, tenderhearted, forgiving one another, even as God for Christ's sake hath forgiven you."*

Through the daily practice of loving, correcting, celebrating, and praying together, our family discovers its God-given purpose, and from that purpose flows an impact that will live far beyond our time on Earth.

Conclusion: A Legacy of Resilience

Living in a multi-generational family is like walking through life with a chorus behind you. Some voices are strong and steady, some are fading with time, and others are just starting to find their rhythm. But together, they create a harmony that carries you through.

We don't keep going just because we're strong; we keep going because we're supported. By memories that remind us where we come from. By love that holds us when life gets heavy. And by legacy—the kind that lives on through stories, traditions, and faith.

Like Hebrews 12:1 says, "*Wherefore seeing we also are compassed about with so great a cloud of witnesses ...*" That cloud isn't just spiritual; it's our family. It's the ancestors who paved the way, the loved ones walking beside us now, and the ones coming up who'll carry the torch. Their presence gives us the strength to keep moving, even when the road gets rough.

And Psalm 145:4 reminds us, "One generation shall praise thy works to another, and shall declare thy mighty acts." That's what we do. We pass it down. Not just the stories, but the spirit. The faith. The love. That's how we keep the melody going.

Because we choose to keep our faith through trials, the next generation learns that strength is not just shown in power but in patience and trust in God. When our children witness us praying, healing, and standing firm, they begin to understand what it truly means to lead with integrity and compassion. They carry forward not just our stories but the values that shaped those stories: faithfulness, accountability, and courage. In this way, our family's resilience becomes a guiding example for how they will govern their own lives and communities in the future.

> As the Lord commands in Deuteronomy 6:6-7: *"And these words, which I command thee this day, shall be in thine heart: And thou shalt teach them diligently unto thy children, and shalt talk of them when thou sittest in thine house, and when thou walkest by the way, and when thou liest down, and when thou risest up."*

Our family will continue to stand as living proof that God's legacy endures from generation to generation, faithfully guiding, shaping, and inspiring all who come after us.

Prayer

Father, thank You for bringing us together and revealing Your hand in the generations of families You have called to rule, nurture, and reflect Your Kingdom on Earth. As You planned before the foundation of the world, may families walk in Your design, demonstrating love, faith, wisdom, and purpose in all they do. I speak over every generation, declaring they will take their rightful place first with You and then within their families, living fully in the blessings You have set before them. Show Your love to each person as they reflect on Your goodness, reminding them that they are deeply blessed in the family You have chosen for them and that You are always working all things for their good. Father, speak to their hearts, guide their minds, and seal this prayer in the precious blood of Jesus, that it will bear lasting fruit now and forevermore. Amen, Amen, and Amen.

Maria Bristol-Reed began her true, intimate walk with the Lord in her early thirties. Her passion is to share the love of Christ with all she encounters because she desires to see others win by fully evolving into who God has created them to be. Maria is a native of Baltimore Maryland and has resided in Charlotte North Carolina for the past 14 years where she has grown tremendously in ministry. She is married to Dante Reed, and between the two of them, they have 5 children and 11 grandchildren.

Was to connect
bristol8091@gmail.com
https://info8556326.wixsite.com/mariascreations

9

GRACE

To Sow into The Lives of Others

Drs. Hiram and Joronda Crawford

Created to Sow

The Bible says that we are made in the image of God: *"So God created man in his own image, in the image of God created he him; male and female created he them"* (Genesis 1:27).

So, what does it mean to be created in the image of God? Let's look at God in the beginning. That will tell us about Him and help us know more about ourselves and others. God created the Heaven and the Earth. This showed that God enjoyed purpose, productivity, activity, and beauty. We also enjoy those things.

God created mankind. This demonstrated that God wanted relationships and love. We also desire relationships and love.

Additionally, God desired to redeem His people, so He sent his only begotten Son. Likewise, we desire redemption, and after our redemption, we desire to see others redeemed.

Because we bear God's image, we are designed to love and to labor into the lives of others. Sowing grace is our governance assignment to form future generations. Will it require sacrifice? Yes! Will it sometimes be a challenge? Absolutely. But it is oh, so worth it. From this day forward, let us step into a life of sowing into the lives of others.

Our Being Made in The Image of God Impacts Us the Most

The two things that impact children, youth, and adults alike are feeling loved and having a sense of purpose as God did and we do. Basically, people make us feel loved, and productive activities give us a sense of purpose. We can all reach out and provide both of these to those around us. We need to ask ourselves what more we can do to help those around us feel loved. We can also ask ourselves what productive activities we can provide that will help those around us know that they have purpose.

> "*The liberal soul shall be made fat: and he that watereth shall be watered also himself*" (Proverbs 11:25).

This book is addressed to all of us because all of us have the opportunity to be a blessing in the lives of others on an ongoing basis. My husband and I have been blessed by so many people throughout our lives—so much so that we decided to try to bless those people by taking them out to dinner. There were so many that we decided to do a banquet to honor all of them at the same time. We selected a place, purchased gifts, and had a marvelous time. The honorees included a fifth-grade teacher, a choir director, a master's degree college professor, a doctoral professor, and of course our parents as well as many others. Each of them had sown into our lives in a special way. In this chapter, we will share how people have sown into our lives. We will also share how we have seen others spend the time to reach out and touch others in very impactful ways. The goal is that each of us will be more inspired to sow into the lives of others and grace their lives, making an eternal difference and impact.

What Sowing Grace Looks Like

Three Short Principles of Sowing Grace

1. Love – God is love, and all mentoring and sowing should be based on love: the kind of love that God shows.
2. Presence – You can't have a real impact on anyone unless you make yourself available and have presence in their life.
3. Excellence – People believe in you when you do things with a spirit of excellence.

Portraits of Sowers

School

More Than Choir Directors

"And let us not be weary in well doing: for in due season, we shall reap, if we faint not" (Galatians 6:9).

Love notices the "troubled kid" and arranges rides. Constance Butts (Connie) was a wonderful example of someone who poured her life into others. As a principal, I often said that any adult could change a child's life for the better and make them want to come to school. She was one such person. They didn't have to be a teacher or counselor. They could be a lunchroom worker, a janitor, or, in this case, a teacher assistant. Connie took on the job of directing the choir. She didn't just take in the "good kids" but seemed to thrive on the troubled kids. The children LOVED her because she loved THEM. Often, she would have the children meet her at her house to assure that they could get to a weekend engagement. When the children in her classroom were in an assembly, she would bring extra barrettes and comb their hair to assure that they looked their best. She literally turned around many a child's life through her love and concern.

Mr. Irvin Bunton was a choir director who affected both of our lives. Mr. Bunton directed Dr. Hiram's Englewood High School Choir in Chicago. During his tenure, he exposed his students to many performance opportunities at churches and concert halls. He had to get permission from parents because his students had rehearsal before school at seven o'clock in the morning.

Mr. Bunton was also the director of the All-City Chicago Choir, of which Dr. Joronda was a part in high school. He promoted excellence at every level and led the choir on many occasions. There was a sectional director for each of the parts (soprano, alto, tenor, bass). After the separate rehearsals, Mr. Bunton would bring them together in perfect harmony. He was the glue that brought perfect accord.

At his retirement, as Hiram Crawford and Joronda Strong entered the room, he prophesied, "A marriage made in Heaven." And so it was!!!

Teachers Who Made a Difference

Wow! What can we say about Jenny Kirby? She was Joronda's fifth-grade teacher and by far her favorite of all her teachers. Jenny Kirby did everything she could to make learning both fun and challenging. She had a back room behind her room. Many play rehearsals and special projects took place in that room. Everyone in her room knew that she loved them and she would go to bat for her students, even challenging their parents.

Church

Ministers Who Made a Difference

> *"Or ministry, let us wait on our ministering: or he that teacheth, on teaching;"* (Romans 12:7).

Elder Claude Christopher made a tremendous difference in Dr. Hiram's life. Hiram's dad was sent to Chicago by the Bishop. Hiram was not at all happy about it. He had to leave his friends.

He could not attend the prestigious high school to which he had been accepted. Elder Claude Christopher befriended him and helped him to change his mind. Elder Christopher's method was that he would spend time with Dr. Hiram as he completed the many chores given by Pastor Crawford, his father. Dr. Hiram had to carry the coal from the truck in the alley to the coal bin in the basement. He also had to stoke the furnace, clean out the clinkers, and pull out the ashes throughout the winter months. Dr. Hiram had to clean the church—sweep, mop, clean the seats, clean the bathroom, and so on. Throughout all of these tasks, Elder Christopher would help him. Elder Christopher used these times to counsel Dr. Hiram.

Dr. Dorothy Sutton Branch, the then-pastor of Commonwealth Community Church, instilled leadership in Dr. Joronda at an early age. When she and her friend were in junior high school, Dr. Branch had them literally running the children's church. She had pastors to preach, but Joronda and Pam ran the entire operation. Dr. Branch even had them be a part of board meetings. What a visionary on developing leadership. Additionally, she went through the trouble to set up religious instruction once a week for the school across the street, which I, Joronda, attended. Students would be dismissed early, and she would teach the classes herself.

Mr. Carlos Jones was the drama director at Commonwealth Community Church. Since I, Dr. Joronda, was an only child, my parents selected the house that they bought because it was across the street from the school and down the street from the church. Therefore, I was able to easily participate in activities in both. Mr. Jones had many drama club rehearsals before Christmas and Easter. The presentations were always sunrise Christmas and

Easter services. What fun it was to prepare for the plays, and the excitement of the presentations was wonderful. The result was that children and families attended early morning services.

Higher Education

Professors Who Made a Difference

When I, Dr. Hiram, worked at Argonne National Laboratory in the 1960s and 1970s, we would have leading scientists from across the nation come to us during the summer so that we could update them on the latest research. We worked on many national projects, like the Apollo program and the moon rock research. We stayed the entire seventy-two hours ready to do anything we could to help the Apollo 13 mission return safely. One of those scientists was Dr. Berard Gerstien from Ames National Laboratory of Iowa State University. He would try to get me to come to Iowa State University to finish my degree. I would give him many reasons for not going. I finally agreed to go to Iowa State University with him if they would give scholarships so I could bring fifty black students with me. I just knew he could not do it.

That next summer, he surprised me with the scholarships. So, I had my friends help, and we went to almost all the ghetto high schools in Chicago and the suburbs. That summer, we took those students to Iowa State University to receive tutoring to bring them up to college level. Most of those students received their degree. I graduated with my degree also. While at Iowa State University, we were able to have our church fellowship with the Ames Iowa Methodist Church. We had many of our children visit the families of the Iowa farmers, and many of them said they did not know where eggs and milk came from.

Dr. Phillis Conningham at Northern Illinois University: I had several friends who tried to get me to enroll, which I finally did. We were able to attend classes in Chicago for the first few classes. The master's degree program at Northen Illinois University was very good and made us work hard. While at that university, I got married. After graduating with my master's degree, I was able to start working on my doctoral degree. While working on that, I was able to travel to Finland and Russia. I was part of a United Nations program called Futures in Education. We met at several universities in Finland and Russia. In Russia, we had a high government official as our guide. As UN representatives, we stayed in some of the best hotels and had some of the best accommodations. Our Russian diplomat showed us her villa in the beautiful mountains. We were able to visit Saint Petersburg galleries, museums, and historical sites, and I was impressed with all the gold in the displays. The conference rooms were royal classics.

The Lord blessed us on the bus ride from Saint Petersburg to Moscow—we prayed for the many churches we passed, and we were able to pass out many gospel tracks. Our Lord Jesus blessed me to meet a Jesus People bus in the Russian town of Vita Kevi. The bus pulled up just in time for me to overhear them say, "We are running out of gospel tracks." I just happened to have a suitcase full of gospel tracks. What a mighty God we serve.

Dr. Grace Dawson was a professor in Dr. Joronda's master's program that had a major impact in her life. Joronda loved teaching and wanted to make a difference in the lives of her students. She was only in the master's program because of encouragement from others and because of lane advancement. She had no interest in becoming an administrator. She must have shared this fact with Dr. Dawson, who replied to her, "If you can make a difference in thirty children's lives (that was the class size at that time), then what about thirty times thirty? That statement, along with the wonderful leadership of her then-principal Hulon Johnson, convinced her that she should take the plunge into administration.

So Many Others

I feel like the writer of Hebrews: *"And what shall I more say? for the time would fail me to tell of Gedeon, and of Barak, and of Samson, and of Jephthae; of David also, and Samuel, and of the prophets"* (Hebrews 11:32).

This chapter would become a book if we told of all of the people who have impacted us—relatives, friends, colleagues, employees, church members, and many others. All of these have been faithful in sowing grace into our lives. May we and you be faithful to Our Lord and Savior Jesus Christ in sowing grace into this generation, the next generation, and many generations to come.

The Harvest Generation Outcomes

> *"One generation shall praise thy works to another, and shall declare thy mighty acts"* (Psalm 145:4).

The Possible Consequences Are Boundless

Only God knows how sowing into the lives of others will impact them. We often say to others that God has a destiny for each of us that we can't imagine if we follow His plan. Helping others find their destiny and sowing into others can have generational impact.

- It can increase higher educational persistence.
- It can improve vocational excellence.
- It can encourage salvation and church continuity.
- It can result in reconciled families.

Call to Action and Prayer of Commission

With God's leading, step into your role as a human developer, sowing into the lives of others. Make a commitment this month to identify one child, youth, or adult to begin your journey sowing grace into the life of another. Be loving. Be present. Do it with consistency and excellence.

Drs. Hiram & Joronda Crawford - married for 33 years. Hiram, a retired computer science department chair; Joronda a retired principal. They co-direct the 40-year-old Pro-Life Pro-Family Coalition, an organization that teaches the importance of pro-life and building a strong biblical family in the black community. They are co-founders of the Faith-Based Credit Union Alliance, which services 33 credit unions nationwide. They have taught weekly computer classes for 30 years to homeless men and women at Pacific Garden Mission. They are board members of several organizations. Most importantly, they love Jesus and attribute all of their success to the Lord and His guidance.

10

IN THE NAME OF LOVE

Timothy Cannon

I grew up in a small town with a population of less than 2,500 people. For a few years, I lived in a two-bedroom house with my parents and five siblings. We didn't have much financially at the time, but we had each other. We received government assistance that helped provide us with food when we needed it. We always saw our parents working and helping other people. We were never told to get good grades in school or to listen to our teachers. Somehow, we just knew that it was expected, and we did it.

As a father to four sons, I am quite concerned about things I have seen and continue to see regarding the way children are prepared to be self-sufficient adults. I have coached two of my sons in sports and have seen the looks on parents' faces when their child does not get enough playing time in a game. I was once confronted by a parent who informed me after a game that her son should have been allowed more time to play because his extended family had come to see him. I wasn't asked to provide a reason for my decision; I was simply told that it should have been different.

This scenario leads me into what I would like to share regarding the messages that we give our children without realizing the damage we may be causing.

This chapter is titled "In the Name of Love" because I believe that most parents who do things for their children do so because they believe it is the loving thing to do. To do something for anyone out of love, one must first know what is best for the other person. Most people do not have the other person's best interest in mind when doing something that would qualify as an act of love. Unfortunately, the focus is too often on how the act will be perceived by others—"if I do something for my child or friend."

Society has perpetuated a myth that if one person does something out of love, and the receiver is appreciative, then whenever that action is repeated, it's always a loving gesture. Being considerate of other people is always a loving gesture. Giving someone a gift, however, may not be. It really depends on the motive behind the action.

Parents should use wisdom when doing things for a child because children process information differently from adults. If a parent gives a child something, the child will think that it's okay for them to have that thing and that there's no reason they should ever be without it—because "my parent gave it to me, and I know they love me." So, when I give my child something they want *before* completing a task, even though I told them they could have it *after* completing it, I have started down a path that could lead the child to expect certain things without meeting the requirements for receiving them.

I had a coworker who told me of a time he bought tickets for his child to see a show that featured *Sesame Street* characters. He said that for hours leading up to the show, his child was not exhibiting the right behavior, so he chose not to take his child to the show.

At first, I was shocked because I thought about the money that had already been spent, but then I realized that the money spent on those tickets was nothing compared to the valuable lesson he taught his child. Too often, parents prioritize their own feelings and circumstances to the detriment of properly training their children to be productive citizens.

Many parents get caught in the trap of trying to provide things for their children that they lacked or wished they had in their own childhood. Many of the things we didn't have were related to pleasure and convenience. Now, there are numerous convenient ways to try and make ourselves happy. We continue to chase this fleeting idea of happiness while more people are faced with depression and mental illness.

The following statement is not a clinical diagnosis, but it is based on my own experience: I suspect that many of those who are depressed have sought happiness in things and discovered that happiness cannot be found in things.

There are so many messages on the radio, TV, and social media that tell us what to do to be happy: Eat at this restaurant, wear these clothes, watch this movie, treat yourself to something nice. Too many adults and children have subscribed to the narrative that a person can make themselves happy by continually indulging in "feel good" activities.

We don't hear many messages that tell us happiness is a choice, because that doesn't encourage people to spend their money on things they don't need. We found ways to be happy without a lot of material possessions because our parents didn't have the resources to play the "let's make ourselves happy" game—or they were wise enough to know that happiness couldn't be found in things.

I have found no verse in the Bible that indicates happiness can be achieved from possessing a particular physical item. The Bible also does not equate happiness with pleasure. Most of the verses I see in Scripture connect happiness with making a choice—choices that result in a good outcome for one or more people.

I absolutely hate the phrase "You, I, or they deserve to be happy." In contrast, I appreciate the phrase "Be happy."

The word "deserve" in the first statement implies that my means to achieve happiness are justified and that no one has the right to question my actions because the goal is happiness. This mindset leaves the door open for a person to indulge in actions that may be unethical, illegal, or even irreversible in the pursuit of happiness.

Martin Luther King Jr. stated that "the pursuit of happiness is one of our inalienable rights." Just because something is a "right" legally does not mean it is "right" biblically.

In contrast, the phrase "Be happy" makes it clear that happiness is a choice that we can make—and that no conditions or possessions are required.

I remember when I first heard about sports teams for children where every child would get a trophy for participating. I also remember how sad and upset I was as I considered the implications of such a mindset and how it could affect children and how they saw the world.

Over ten years later, the results are worse than I could have imagined. I thought this might only affect competitive sports, but it has spread much farther. The "everyone gets a trophy" mindset expanded into the classroom through the *No Child Left Behind* policy, which advanced children to the next grade even though they hadn't met the minimum performance standards of the previous one.

This same mindset has now entered the workforce, where too many young adults expect promotion to management after only a few years on the job.

What's worse is that this generation has been raised to believe that work is a necessary evil—a means to an end—rather than a part of life that builds discipline, skill, and purpose.

Now, we face a major challenge in the workforce related to "work-life balance" because children have been trained to expect balance before learning endurance. Children haven't been taught that *work is a part of life*; they've been taught that work is simply what you do to get money to do other things.

Final message to parents and those responsible for the training of children:

Tell them as much truth as you believe they can handle, and they will let you know when it's too much. The truths we keep from our children only create distrust.

If you don't want to explain something to your child, tell them that you don't want to talk about it and provide a clear and honest reason. Don't tell them it's "none of their business," because they may already know more than you think.

If a child asks you something, and you don't know the answer, let them know that you don't—but help them find the answer or someone who does know. Kids know when adults don't know.

> The Bible says, "*Train up a child in the way he should go: and when he is old, he will not depart from it*" (Proverbs 22:6).

Therefore, we should teach children to be honest—to say what they mean and mean what they say. Children should be taught that there are consequences when they don't follow the rules instead of receiving a pass because we don't want to hurt their feelings or see them cry.

Parents must remember that children will one day reach an age where they are responsible for their own decisions. If they are never allowed to make decisions, how will they develop the wisdom required to function as an adult?

There are too many grown-aged children who are overly dependent on parents and other adults. The real problem is that these grown-aged children don't realize their deficiency because dependency has been their normal. One potential outcome is that the parent becomes frustrated with the child's lack of development. Another is that the child, realizing the control, rebels—leaving home to prove independence only to return frustrated and unprepared.

Impacting a Generation

As we reflect on what it truly means to *love* our children, we must remember that love without truth leads to entitlement, and truth without love leads to rebellion. Impacting a generation begins with reintroducing accountability, discipline, and faith back into the name of love.

Every act of parenting, teaching, and mentoring must point children toward purpose, not comfort. When we correct, we shape character; when we withhold out of wisdom, we cultivate endurance; when we tell the truth, we build trust.

This is how we impact a generation—not by giving them everything we didn't have but by teaching them Who they cannot live without.

> *"And now abideth faith, hope, charity, these three; but the greatest of these is charity"* (1 Corinthians 13:13).

In the name of love, may we raise a generation that governs their hearts, their homes, and their habits with grace and truth.

Timothy Cannon is from Drew, MS. When he was 12 years old, his family moved to Georgia. He lived in Georgia until he graduated from Southwest Dekalb High School in Decatur, GA and Tuskegee University. He is an Air Force veteran. He has been married for 26 years and has four sons. He lives in Charlotte, NC.

11

THE HEALING GRACE OF HOME

Shanna Neal

WARNING: THE FOLLOWING QUESTIONS MAY RESULT IN TRIGGERS OR REVISITING TRAUMA.

Do you remember what you were like before you were afraid for the first time? Who were you before your first disappointment or learned expectations of others? Do you remember? Do you recall your first memory of fear, uncertainty, confusion, wounding, or distrust? Have you ever felt the pain of having your heart broken—shattered—and what feels like an irreparable wound with no undo button? Be careful not to draw a conclusion that this place is limited to betrayal or a willful action of another.

Do you know what it means, or have you had the experience of "going to the bottom of the pond" with a friend or "climbing into the casket" with an individual who feels swallowed up by grief and darkness? To "just going there," where the depths of pain, brokenness, and the lowest places of another's life isn't about you at all?

Do you know the healing touch of beauty in your ashes? Do you know the feeling of oil or salve being massaged into places within your life or circumstances where no words seem adequate to describe? Yes, to know this place in your own life but also in the burden-bearing of another's life, and to bring a sense of home that expresses, "You are not alone." Only as we have experienced Immanuel (God With Us) in our lives can we emanate this loving expression in the lives of others.

This chapter aims to explore areas such as these and remind us that we are first and foremost spirit, and we have a soul and live in a body that is just a dusty frame housing so many more complex parts.

> *"And the Lord God formed man of the dust of the ground, and breathed into his nostrils the breath of life; and man became a living soul"* (Genesis 2:7).

We became alive through the very breath of God. The Apostle Paul tells us in Acts 17:28 "*For in him we live, and move, and have our being.*"

I often wonder what it must have been like in the relationship between God, the man, and the woman as they knew the purest of communion in the garden of Eden before sin entered the picture. What was spirit-to-Spirit communion like with no interference of doubt, unbelief, fear, confusion, anxiety, or even disappointment? A place of oneness with our Father God in knowing full safety, security, and significance as His creation must have been a glorious Eden of Heaven on Earth. The *knowing communion* of this glory alone, between God and mankind, even with God's boundary and forbiddance of partaking from the tree that would give way to the knowledge of good and evil, seems to provoke more questions. How long did they get to experience this glory of Heaven on Earth with God before choosing something far different? If we were Adam or Eve, how long would we have held out before crossing the boundary of disobedience? Yet mankind's curiosity, doubt, disobedience, and naive submission to a perverse deceiver opened up the closure of this glory, like the beginning of an end, of what was once our boundless intimate fellowship with our Creator.

In the Father's love for us and the revealing of the humility of His character, God gave His creation of mankind the gift of choice, all the while giving boundaries with consequences of our choosing. At one time, mankind knew the love of the Father as well as His protection and security without the clutter of troubling circumstances, resulting in our own self-motivated survival strategies interfering with the relationship. Jesus, as the Way to the Father, the Truth of the Father, and the only Life in the Father, became everything we need to restore this relationship.

Jesus is the WAY home, the TRUTH of what home is, and the only LIFE-line to receive home.

> *"I am the way, the truth, and the life: no man cometh unto the Father, but by me"* (John 14:6).

The one and only TRUE Son of God came to show us the way home and restore our sonship to the Father. The idea of home, family, and relationship was always God's. The work of restoration in God always points to the original intention of God and is not merely returning something backward to its former condition. God has more in mind for us than us navigating life on our own, more than we could ever imagine.

I submit to you, dear reader, that home is not merely a place, but our home is in Him. We are a spirit that was created for home. Our spirit wants to trust, love, receive unconditional love, and experience an intimacy with our Father through the work of His Spirit. So, what's our part now? How do we get home? How do we experience the healing that home provides? Where is home for us? How do we obtain this, explore this, grow in this, and allow others to experience through us? Unfortunately, on this side of Heaven, there is a fight involved both internally and externally in achieving this gift that God has provided. The fight within our very nature is a part of it, and then there is the wager of our enemy that is deceiving, scheming, manipulating, and executing our destruction with every possible opportunity available. How does this factor into receiving what God so graciously promises to provide of healing as the children's bread (Matthew 15:26)?

The healing of being home and experiencing true life is for every person who is ready to return home and believes, confesses, and receives Jesus Christ as the new Lord of their life. No matter how long we have or have not believed in God, attended church, or recited prayers at the direction of others, Jesus doesn't invade our lives without being invited in.

> *"Behold, I stand at the door, and knock: if any man hear my voice, and open the door, I will come in to him, and will sup with him, and he with me"* (Revelation 3:20).

This healing experience, which begins with being born again and coming alive to God, while it is for everyone, many stop short at a new believer's prayer and miss what it means to find our lives in the *one relationship worth dying for.*

> *"He that findeth his life shall lose it: and he that loseth his life for my sake shall find it"* (Matthew 10:39).
>
> *"For ye are dead, and your life is hid with Christ in God"* (Colossians 3:3).

After all, what we are being invited into is a NEW relationship with our Father through His Son, Jesus Christ. There is so much to discover, learn, know, and grow into. Healing of the soul begins with this, and there is simply no other way to know this healing without inviting the Healer to come in and live in us.

> *"But he that is joined unto the Lord is one spirit"* (I Corinthians 6:17).

The story of the two sons in Luke 15 contrasts what it means to know about home—even live in the home with the Father—

and never experience or receive the fullness of what the Father provides. There is one son who left home and walked away from the covering and protection of the Father's house and another son who never physically left home but wasn't experiencing the true benefits and healing that home provided.

One son took his inheritance and left to find his own way, until famine and hitting rock bottom shook him back to what he discovered he had lost. He knew enough of the Father's house to decide to return, if only to settle into being a servant.

> *"And when he came to himself, he said, How many hired servants of my father's have bread enough and to spare, and I perish with hunger! I will arise and go to my father, and will say unto him, Father, I have sinned against heaven, and before thee, And am no more worthy to be called thy son: make me as one of thy hired servants"* (Luke 15:17-19).

The son who never left home discovered his brother's return and resented the celebration that the Father brought and the restoration and healing that came with it for his brother. What he believed and experienced in the relationship with their father, even while remaining at home, being a son, wasn't quite enough to withstand or prevent the bitterness, resentment, unforgiveness, and maybe even feelings of injustice that arose in his heart in the face of celebration.

> *"And he said unto him, Son, thou art ever with me, and all that I have is thine"* (Luke 15:31).

This is the real premise and heart of this chapter, which I titled "The Healing Grace of Home."

This passage reminds me of Genesis 27:36-38, where another story of two sons unravels, with a son (Jacob) who deceived his father into giving a firstborn blessing and a very heartbroken Esau who is crying out to his father Isaac after learning that his brother Jacob has stolen the blessing reserved for him as a firstborn. *"And Esau said unto his father, Hast thou but one blessing, my father? bless me, even me also, O my father. And Esau lifted up his voice and wept"* (Genesis 27:38). Of course, Isaac, however, has already given the primary blessing to Jacob, leaving him with only a partial one for Esau, which he gives.

How many believers in Jesus seemed to be in the house and are not experiencing the *"healing of home"*? For the sake of this work, I am defining home as where our purpose and lives originated, where we experience belonging and believing the truth about who we really are and were created to be.

> *"I am my beloved's, and my beloved is mine"* (Solomon 6:3).

Jesus showed us how to be one with the Father in such a way that He only did what the Father desired or willed. I believe many of us "want to want" this oneness when it comes to our relationship with God that will bring the outcomes we may truly desire. However, the competition with what our flesh desires and the wrestling match within our soul that rages between our thoughts, feelings, and self-centered will mean that many of us give up or give in prematurely.

I want to share an abbreviated poetic version of my journey, the healing of home.

Oh the joy of this salvation,
as I journey down a whole new road.

With the thought that each room in my heart's house
was a full lock and load.

With all the faith and courage needed
to run this race of grace,

Until just like Jesus, the Spirit led me into my own
desert to be tempted, to see which direction I'd take.

A series of hills of challenges of fear for my children
showed me there were holes

And wounds of unbelief in hidden places of my heart's
house, where I didn't let anyone go.

There were valleys of sorrow,
new acquaintances with names like grief.

Could this still be the Spirit leading me,
or is it the one named Thief?

I thought, how will I ever find
the strength to start a climb

To the mountain of the Lord before me?

Would I ever know Him as healer, deliverer,
or rescuer of mine?

None of this journey was anything
like I thought I'd see,

But then I met death, and I thought,
"Will it be him or me"?

This new mystery of death wasn't a person but a place,

And at this table were servings of things
for which I had no taste.

Beverages of suffering served in cups labeled
"My Grace,"

Of which I wanted no part, but as I watched others
drink, something else happened that day.

It wasn't written in ink, or labels, or charts,

But the words "is sufficient for you"
became cradled around the heart.

Not just one, but of each person who slowly took a drink

At this sacred table of the Master,
whose very death made us think.

Oh, this sobering table of the Lord
on this journey of grace,

Where all are given the same opportunity
of sacrificed space.

Will we love our life and hold on to it?

And for this, we lose.

Or we acquaint with the One who went first,
who redeemed us,

And lay it down.

We must choose.

This race of grace, for this I've laid down all,

But what is to be gained cannot be counted small!

For Him I will live; for Him I will die,

And all to behold Him and the look in His Eye!

Suffering and Surrender, to my surprise, became allies.

But the biggest win of all is Jesus My Prize.

By God's Grace, I've found Home!

Shanna M. Neal, born and raised in Chicago, Illinois, she completed her undergraduate studies at ORU and worked vocationally in education, social work, and administration. A full-time call into ministry led her to pursue graduate studies and to serve in team pastoring with her husband in South Bend, Indiana. She is the author of HeartWork: From a House of Sand to One That Stands and leads the HeartWork & Soul Care ministry.

www.shannmneal.com

SECTION IV: KINGDOM GOVERNANCE

12

GRACED TO ENGAGE

Doug Neal

Through the creation story found in the first three chapters of the book of Genesis, we see that God created us for relationships. He desires to know us and for us to know Him. Not to mention, He desires for us to know one another while being at the center of our human connection. To make any relationship work, whether human or divine, it takes an intentional effort of engagement. One important ingredient in such engagement is understanding who we are and how the other person's life relates to our own.

This is why it is imperative for us to understand our relationship to God in accordance with the way He functions. There are several identifiable ways in which God moves and functions, all of which give us a definitive way in which we respond to Him. This chapter will discuss four of those functions along with the distinct ways we are to respond to Him.

The first function of God that we want to focus on is God as Father. After this, we will look at God's function as Master, followed by His function as King and concluding with His function as Creator. To help us examine these functions, we will use a fourfold metaphor of a house, land, a Kingdom, and the world. These four backdrops, or themes, with the addition of various Bible passages will help us understand and further develop our relationship with the Lord and others.

We Live in a House ...

It is impossible to overemphasize how deeply God cherishes His relationship with His people. The details of creation throughout the beginning chapters of Genesis reveal God's inherent nature toward relationships and intimacy. These chapters also highlight God's desire for family. God values family immensely.

Though man's sin separated us from God, His redemptive plan through the death, burial, and resurrection of Jesus Christ restored man's privilege to have dominion over the works of His hands. But more than this, the original intent of the relationship between God and man was also restored. Man could once again delight in fellowship with God through the indwelling of the Holy Spirit.

Our fourfold metaphor begins with us as believers and followers of Christ Jesus living together with God in a "house." In this house, God is Father, which subsequently positions us as sons and daughters relating to Him. As sons and daughters of the same Father, this of course makes us brothers and sisters in Christ, relating to one another accordingly.

The overarching theme of the "house" level is family and intimacy. Family indicates an inborn connection that comes with our existence. When we're born into a family, it's not a choice. It's simply the result of our birth. With family comes intimacy. Intimacy is the relational agreement to be thoroughly honest in sharing who we are with each other while also respecting, protecting, and embracing each other as we share our open hearts.

In the house, the family meets in two places—at the feet of Jesus and at the table of the Lord. In Luke 10, we read the familiar story of Mary and Martha. These two sisters, along with their brother Lazarus, were dear friends of Jesus. When Jesus and His disciples came to have dinner with them, Martha became very busy preparing the meal, while Mary sat at the feet of Jesus. Martha eventually became frustrated and complained to Jesus to have Mary come and help her in the kitchen. But Jesus reproved her, saying, "Martha, Martha, thou art careful and troubled about many things: But one thing is needful: and Mary hath chosen that good part, which shall not be taken away from her" (Luke 10:41-42).

There are several lessons to take away from this moment. But in conjunction with our metaphor, Martha's issue was not her busyness. It was her timing. Jesus did not correct what Martha was doing. He corrected her attitude. And why was her attitude off? She may have encountered this frustration because she was not properly responding to Jesus.

While Jesus wanted to pour out His heart to those at His feet, Martha was more concerned with preparing His meal. Mary, on the other hand, got the timing right. As Jesus poured out, she was ready to receive. Martha was instead trying to do her own pouring, which clashed with how Jesus was functioning in the moment. Everyone certainly needed to eat, but there's a time for preparing a meal and a time to sit and listen.

The engagement level shifts once things move to the table. Jesus is talking, and everyone else is quietly listening. As Jesus speaks, everyone at His feet receives something different. When we move to the table, we all bring with us what we received at the feet of Jesus. Everything given to us is a gift from the Lord and is laid out on the table for everyone to enjoy. At Jesus' feet, He is talking, and everyone else is listening. But at the table, there is a wonderful cacophony of conversation between everyone. And everyone is feasting on what the Father has freely provided.

At the table, there's a whole cornucopia of delightful items to partake of from prophecy to marriage, from wisdom to humility, and from thanksgiving to discernment, generosity, peace, submission, worship, forgiveness, love, kindness, faith, and the list goes on. What may be closely located and easily accessed by one person at the table may be a far reach for someone else. That means they will have to ask for assistance from someone else at the table if they want to partake in what is out of reach.

Like at a Thanksgiving feast; I might be able to reach the mashed potatoes but need assistance from someone to pass the gravy. Likewise, I may understand the depths of prophecy but lack humility. I may need someone else's help to get the lessons of being humble. The same way mashed potatoes taste better with gravy, my prophetic word will taste much better when I add humility to it.

The House Is on Land ...

The house is a very pleasant place to abide; it is filled with loving interactions between us and God as well as between each other. The fullness of the house is plotted on "land." Land in this metaphor represents the realm of authority that we have been granted by God that is outside of the house but still within the scope of our family. On the land, God functions as Master, and we respond to Him as His faithful servants. We also respond to each other as co-laborers in Christ.

In the Parable of the Talents in Matthew 25, a man with three servants leaves his house and bestows his goods to these three servants. To one, he gave five talents; to another, he gave two talents, and to the third, he gave one talent. The first two servants multiplied their talents, but the last of the three servants went and hid his talent. When the master returned, he commended and rewarded the first two as faithful servants, but the third servant who buried his one talent was scolded and thrown out, having his one talent remitted to the servant with five talents.

The master of the house looked favorably on the first two servants because they applied the overarching theme of the land—work. The "land" level is where assignments along with positions, accompanied by coinciding authority and anointing, are given to individuals. Work has been the assignment of mankind since the beginning. In Genesis 2:15, God placed man in the Garden of Eden to tend and keep it. Part of our earthly assignment is to understand and steward what God has created and called us to tend and keep. With this comes the responsibility to work together with others, submit to authority, release our gifts, and execute within our assignment to produce the Kingdom results God desires.

Another passage that describes our engagement, particularly with each other on this "land" level, is found in 1 Corinthians 3. The Apostle Paul describes his efforts alongside that of Apollos, a co-laborer and fellow minister of the Gospel, as that of companion workers in God's field. Paul says in verse 6, "I have planted, Apollos watered; but God gave the increase." Paul continues in verse 9, saying, "For we are labourers together with God: ye are God's husbandry…"

What we discover here is that God's people are in essence the land. We are where the work is being done. We are where the seeds are being sown. And we are where the fruit is being produced. Paul concludes this verse by saying, "Ye are God's building." So, we see that we are also where God lives. As Paul says in 1 Corinthians 6:19, we are "… the temple of the Holy Ghost which is in you." The assignments, gifts, and authority that we are given pertain to how we help each other to spiritually grow, draw closer to God, love others, and live for God's purpose.

Our engagement as co-laborers on the land does not replace our bond of love, family, and intimacy in the house. It builds upon it. The love and intimacy we experience as family in the house help us to work together on the land. This is why the body of Christ always needs to have safe spaces for people to share their lives intimately. Our efforts toward discipleship must not be limited to assignments and responsibilities. They must also include relational bonding with God and with others.

The Land Is in a Kingdom ...

Like natural families, the family of God increases in size. Acts 2 speaks of the Church having 3,000 people added to its number as the Lord continued to add to the Church daily. This numerical growth continues today. Jesus' purpose for coming to this world was so that those outside of the family of God could be welcomed in. This is the primary focus of the next phase of our metaphor—the Kingdom.

With our figurative house being on land, the next place we examine in our metaphor is the land being in a Kingdom. The first two phases of this metaphor pertained to our engagement with God and others within the body of Christ. As we look at the realm of the Kingdom phase, this is where we begin to venture out into the rest of the world. In the Kingdom, God is, of course, King. In fact, He is King of all kings and Lord of all lords. But our engagement with God on this level is not as simple as with those on the land. On this level, we rule and reign together with God, seated in heavenly places with our King. On this level, we are kings, priests, joint-heirs, and more than conquerors.

The theme of the Kingdom level is conquest. We engage in battle but not against people. Ephesians 6:12 says, "For we wrestle not against flesh and blood, but against principalities, against powers, against the rulers of the darkness of this world, against spiritual wickedness in high places." Our mission is to win the lost back to God. To do this, we combat enemy forces by the power of God with His Word, His Spirit, and the precious blood of Jesus.

Paul says in 2 Corinthians 10:3-5, "For though we walk in the flesh, we do not war after the flesh: (For the weapons of our warfare are not carnal, but mighty through God to the pulling down of strong holds;) Casting down imaginations, and every high thing that exalteth itself against the knowledge of God, and bringing into captivity every thought to the obedience of Christ." Through God's power and the arsenal of His Word, His Spirit, and the shed blood of Jesus Christ, we defeat the enemy and retrieve lost souls into the Kingdom of God.

As we present the Gospel to lost souls, we relate to fellow believers as royalty. 1 Peter 2:9 says, "But ye are a chosen generation, a royal priesthood, an holy nation, a peculiar people; that ye should shew forth the praises of him who hath called you out of darkness into his marvellous light." This not only helps us to fight the spiritual warfare of saving souls but also creates a winsome atmosphere that compels others to become a part of God's Kingdom.

The Kingdom Is in a World ...

For the conclusion of our metaphor, we use the world as the resting place for the Kingdom that contains the land upon which the house is built. The world is our wide-angle view, the big picture of how God functions in our lives. In the "world" phase of our metaphor, God is Creator. He is the One who made both Heaven and Earth and is possessor of the same. God made the world and everything in it. The Earth is the Lord's and the fullness thereof, the world and all they that dwell in it.

With God as Creator, we relate to Him as worshippers and to each other as fellow worshippers. Worship is also the theme of this level in our metaphor. We express our worship through words of adoration and acts of worship, such as bowing, kneeling, singing and lifting our hands, and even through sacrificial giving. But the primary way in which we express our worship unto God is through obedience. As the Prophet Samuel admonished King Saul in 1 Samuel 15:22, "... to obey is better than sacrifice."

Worship services are filled with these types of expressions. The Word of God is often spoken accompanied by prophetic words. These expressions are designed to bring people into a place of reverent fear of our Holy God and Creator. When we understand Him as Creator, we understand that He is also the One who can destroy. As Jesus said in Matthew 10:28, "And fear not them which kill the body, but are not able to kill the soul: but rather fear him which is able to destroy both soul and body in hell."

In giving our worship to God, we cancel the fear of man. We worship God unashamedly and give to Him the honor that is due to Him. We give thanks to Him and bless His name. People can only harm us physically, which pales in comparison to what God can do to both the body and the soul. God is always worthy of praise and worship. Neither time restrictions, venues, nor our physical or emotional state should ever be allowed to deter us from reverent worship of our God and Creator. He is the Father of the family of God, the Master of the land, the King of the Kingdom, and the Creator of the world. There is no one else like Him. There is no other God besides Him.

Doug Neal is a Masters graduate in Biblical Studies. He serves as a chaplain in Nappanee, IN. He and his wife, Shanna, also serve as pastors of Christian Life Center South Bend. They are the proud parents of three adult children, and have a passionate drive to foster and promote unity throughout the body of Christ.

13

THE GIFT OF LEADERSHIP

Provides Grace for Entrepreneurship

Neesha Stringfellow

Scripture Reference: Proverbs 18:16 - "Your gift will make room for you and set you before great men."

As a child, I never envisioned myself as a leader or considered that I was called to leadership. Recognizing the gifts, yet they were often overshadowed by feelings of insecurity, rejection, and a lack of self-worth. Looking back, I can trace my path to leadership as far back as age six, when I unknowingly began practicing leadership in my first-grade classroom. I always had a natural inclination to encourage and uplift others, making them feel valued and purposeful, even when I struggled with my own self-belief.

Growing up in a bustling family with so many dynamics including the church environment, a solid foundation being rooted in faith was never in question.

Although my parents provided what they could, I do believe they did not have the capacity to nurture my emerging leadership potential. Like many families, we faced our share of instability, which at times stifled my growth. However, I often found myself drawn to strong leaders and inspired by the gifts I saw others ignite within their communities. It's vital for us to pay attention to the innate gifts of leadership in yourselves, ensuring we don't overlook the moments to nurture and develop these abilities.

As the scripture reminds us, "gifts and callings are without repentance."The scripture reference for "gifts and callings are without repentance" is found in Romans 11:29 (KJV).

Meaning: This verse means that the gifts and callings that God has given us He won't take back. It emphasizes the idea that God's plans and intentions for each person remain, regardless of their choices or actions. Regardless of the dynamics we experience in life, the gifts God places within us are destined to surface. Our hope is that these gifts ultimately bring glory to God rather than serving our own ambitions.

Point One: Acknowledge Your Leadership Gifts

Recognizing the leadership gift within you is crucial. What does this look like? Are you often the one who blazes trails or envisions new projects? If so, I encourage you to seek the Lord and ask, "Lord, have You given me the gift of leadership?"

Point Two: Surround Yourself with Inspirational Leaders

Investing in yourself is essential in understanding your leadership gift. Early on, I sought wise counsel, knowing there was a gift inside me, even if I didn't understand how to utilize it fully. Despite feelings of insecurity, I kept pushing forward, growing in areas I once thought impossible.

At just 18 years old, as the eldest of eight siblings, I felt a responsibility to ensure my brothers and sisters thrived. I began to take initiative alongside my husband, organizing family events, Bible studies, and youth gatherings. I noticed a need and acted on the gift that God had given me, which not only strengthened our family ties but also connected us to a larger community. Surrounding yourself with those who elevate your gifts creates invaluable opportunities for learning and serving, fostering a deeper understanding of your leadership potential.

My leadership gift eventually blossomed into the grace for the entrepreneur.

Growing up being surrounded by strong leaders, I allowed my pain to blind me from recognizing that I was sitting in the midst of a legacy rooted in true entrepreneurship. I discovered that the grace for entrepreneurship was part of my legacy, rooted in my family history. My grandfather, the late Pastor Hiram Crawford, was an entrepreneur—he started grocery stores, founded a credit union that's still thriving, ventured into real estate, and more.

This heritage revealed that entrepreneurship was woven into my identity.

The Gift of Leadership is Graced for Entrepreneurship

Entrepreneurship is defined by Webster's Dictionary as "the activity of setting up a business or businesses, taking on financial risks in the hope of profit." It's more than just making money; it encompasses building a legacy, creating jobs, providing training, and establishing businesses that contribute to the community.

Now, let's explore the word grace. Grace refers to "unmerited favor" or "a gift from God." It embodies kindness, mercy, and the ability to do things you may not feel qualified for. When we talk about grace in the context of entrepreneurship, we acknowledge that it's not just about personal achievement; it's about the divine support that empowers us to lead, inspire, and uplift others.

Entrepreneurship may not always manifest as wealth or financial success; rather, it's about recognizing the gifts in others and helping them uncover their potential, even when they can't see it themselves.

For many years, I didn't acknowledge my own value as a leader. At 22, I opened my first business, and since then, I have launched over ten different ventures and assisted others in their entrepreneurial journeys. There's a significant truth in reproduction; entrepreneurship thrives on producing more leaders and creating opportunities.

Being a leader means you don't have to walk this path alone. You want to uplift others and allow your gift to pave the way for them as well. As my late mentor once told me, "You should have seven streams of income, but you can't run them all by yourself." The grace for entrepreneurship opens doors, revealing possibilities for both you and those around you.

The second point I want to emphasize is: What are you graced for in entrepreneurship? What does that look like in your life? I encourage you to take some time to write down the areas where your gift has made room for you. Reflect on how you have reproduced and blessed others, even if your impact was for a season. Sometimes ventures don't last long, but their influence can be lasting. Consider how many lives were touched and changed while your endeavors were active.

The concept of grace is deeply intertwined with both leadership and entrepreneurship in several meaningful ways:

1. Unmerited Favor: The concept of grace is definitely intertwined with both leadership and entrepreneurship, and I'd like to share the many ways it does this. Grace is God's reflection of favor, which is essential for effective leadership and entrepreneurship. Sometimes, leaders find themselves in situations where they must rely on the support and goodwill of others. Grace enables leaders to inspire trust and loyalty, even in challenging circumstances. However, we can't let the challenges overtake us. It's important to remember that fostering the gift of entrepreneurship—whether in ministry, business, or launching initiatives that can bring about change requires a community and a collaborative effort.

2. Empowerment: Grace allows leaders and entrepreneurs to empower those around them. By recognizing and nurturing

the gifts in others, leaders can create opportunities for their team members to thrive.

3. Growing Pains: Grace acknowledges the inevitability of mistakes. In both leadership and entrepreneurship, setbacks are common. Embracing grace means understanding that failure is part of the journey and can lead to valuable lessons. Leaders who practice grace create a culture where team members feel safe to take risks and learn from their experiences and if they are wise they will take the opportunity to grow from them. Escaping growing pains will cause your dreams to die.
4. Vision and Purpose: The scripture tells us that ... where there is no vision the people perish ... thats why its so important to know you, you are graced for this. Grace inspires you to work toward a greater purpose. While personal gain is a natural desire for many entrepreneurs, we must not let it overshadow our commitment to reach our goals or compromise our values. It's essential to contribute to the obedience and vision of the assignment God has placed on our lives. Remaining aligned with this purpose enhances motivation not only for yourself, but also for the community you serve. People are watching; they may see your vision even if they don't fully understand it. They might witness your journey of purpose and may not always agree, but as you continue to push forward and persevere, you will start to see encouragement rise within the community around you.
5. Resilience: Grace builds resilience, a crucial trait for leaders and entrepreneurs. It provides the fortitude to

persevere through challenges, knowing that support and understanding exist. This resilience can inspire and uplift teams, creating a shared sense of purpose and determination.

In summary, grace enriches leadership and entrepreneurship by enhancing relationships, fostering empowerment, embracing mistakes, promoting inclusivity, aligning with a higher purpose, and cultivating resilience. It transforms the way leaders influence their teams and the impact entrepreneurs have on their communities, ultimately leading to more meaningful connections and contributions.

I challenge you to reflect: Do you have the grace for entrepreneurship? How can you recognize it within yourself?

Neesha Stringfellow, married to Wesley for since 1988. Neesha is a dedicated Executive Director of HeartLife Ministries, a nonprofit focused on community outreach and support. As a Master Coach, author, and Outreach Pastor, she guides individuals and couples toward stronger relationships.

Alongside her husband Wesley, Neesha hosts one of the largest marriage conferences in the Midwest for over 27 years. Neesha organizes programs for children and youth, including holiday traditions and suicide prevention workshops, emphasizing compassion and resilience. Her work addresses mental health and substance use challenges, ensuring every child is seen and valued. Above all, Neesha is committed to glorifying God through her mission of fostering hope and growth in future generations.

14

FROM SERVANT TO SON

Stepping into My True Identity

Dr. Latricia Williams

Have you ever found yourself doing things simply to be rewarded or out of habit, yet you feel no fulfillment after completing the task? Have you ever worked out of obligation instead of purpose, sensing that you're not living up to your fullest potential? If you answered yes, you and I have something in common.

My name is Dr. Latricia Williams, and I have accomplished some significant goals in my life, such as recently obtaining my doctoral degree in theology. I am a certified life coach who specializes in emotional wellness, and I am also a published author.

I love helping others, and throughout my professional career, I've had the honor of serving the elderly population as a social service manager. I always took great pride in serving others; however, in a recent season, I found myself struggling to do what I know I've been called to do, even after assisting so many people and accomplishing so many amazing things. I had been functioning in what was comfortable instead of stepping into my full Identity in God. I often told others, "I am a servant, and I am here to serve," yet I realized that God was calling me higher, to live as His daughter, not merely as His servant.

Understanding Servanthood and Sonship

There is a powerful distinction between being a servant and being a son of God. (Please note that I use "son of God" to mean both sons and daughters of God.) What I have experienced personally is living more like a servant than a son. The difference between the two lies at the very heart of our relationship with the Father. Throughout Scripture, God reveals Himself not only as a Master but as a loving Father who calls His children into intimacy, not performance.

The Parable of the Prodigal Son (Luke 15:11-32) illustrates this transition beautifully. It depicts how one moves from being estranged and from servanthood to restored Sonship through repentance and the Father's love.

Many believers, including myself, unknowingly live as servants in the Father's house rather than as sons, and we unconsciously function out of obligation rather than relationship. When we operate this way, our spiritual battery drains low, and our perspective shifts from intimacy to performance. I want to explain how this distinction is revealed in the prodigal son's journey and how understanding our true Identity brings restoration and purpose.

What Is Servanthood?

Servanthood is the posture of duty. It is often associated with obedience, humility, and submission, and these qualities are good and necessary in the Kingdom of God. Jesus said in Matthew 20:26, *"But whosoever will be great among you, let him be your minister."* Yet, servanthood alone does not define our Kingdom Identity.

A servant obeys out of duty, motivated by reward or fear of punishment. Servants know their master's commands but not necessarily his heart. In my case, my servanthood stemmed from knowing I was good at helping others. Serving comes naturally, and I felt obligated to use this gift or else God might take it away.

In John 15:15, Jesus tells His disciples, *"I call you not servants; for the servants knoweth not what his lord doeth: but I have called you friends."* Servants perform tasks, but they often lack intimacy. Their relationship is transactional and rooted in work rather than inheritance.

What Is Sonship?

Sonship, on the other hand, is the posture of a relationship with the Father. It flows from love, not labor. A son does not serve to earn love; he serves because he is loved. *"For ye have not received the spirit of bondage again to fear; but ye have received the Spirit of adoption, whereby we cry, Abba, Father"* (Romans 8:15).

Confidence, security, and Identity come through Sonship. A son knows his place in the Father's house, and his actions flow from belonging.

The difference between a servant and a son is not necessarily in their work but in their motivation. Servants work *for* approval, but sons work *from* approval.

John 1:12 affirms this truth: *"But as many as received him, to them gave he power to become the sons of God, even to them that believe on his name."* Sonship is not earned; it is received through faith. This divine adoption empowers us to live from Identity, not insecurity.

The Journey of the Prodigal Son

The Parable of the Prodigal Son gives a vivid picture of transformation. The younger son's story mirrors humanity's fall, repentance, and restoration into God's family.

In Luke 15:12, the younger son demands his inheritance and leaves his father's house. This symbolizes humanity's desire for independence, to have God's blessings without His presence. In doing this, the son not only left home but also the relationship that defined his Identity.

As he wandered into a distant country, his spiritual connection faded. Luke 15:14 explains that after everything was spent, a severe famine came. This famine represents the emptiness that comes from disconnection from the Father.

The prodigal son eventually found himself feeding pigs, which is a symbol of impurity and degradation. He became a servant, bound by necessity rather than freedom. This illustrates what happens when we drift from our God-given identity and live beneath our inheritance, mistaking survival for purpose.

The Turning Point and Restoration

The turning point came when the prodigal son *"came to himself"* (Luke 15:17). He remembered the goodness of his Father and decided to return home. The Father didn't receive him as a servant but restored him as a son. When we return to Him, His Spirit rekindles love, purpose, and confidence within us.

Sonship and Generational Legacy

True Sonship doesn't end with personal restoration; it establishes legacy. Sons and daughters of God carry generational impact because they live out of divine Identity. When we embrace Sonship, we become conduits of Kingdom inheritance, passing on faith, wisdom, and spiritual authority to the next generation. Just as Jesus empowered His disciples to continue His work, God calls His sons and daughters to reproduce His nature in others. Legacy flows from identity. Servants may complete assignments, but sons build generations. When we live as sons, our obedience today becomes someone else's freedom tomorrow.

Conclusion

> Living as a son means walking daily in the awareness of the Father's love and authority. Sons rest in the finished work of Christ, while servants strive for acceptance. Galatians 4:7 declares, *"Wherefore thou art no more a servant, but a son; and if a son, then an heir of God through Christ."*

Servants fear punishment; sons rest in forgiveness. Servants work for wages; sons live from inheritance. Servants seek approval; sons know they are already approved. This transformation changes everything. It changes how we worship, how we serve, and how we lead.

Let us live as true sons, who walk in a deep relationship with our Father God. When we live from His love and reflect His heart, we don't just change lives; we shape generations. Our choices, our faith, and our intimacy with the Father become seeds that grow into legacies. So, rise up sons, and walk in your Sonship.

I am **Dr. Latricia Williams**, and my heart's desire is to teach and support others, in developing emotional intelligence so they can experience true emotional wellness. Holding a Ph.D. in Theology, I blend biblical wisdom with practical strategies to help individuals heal, grow, and thrive emotionally.

Connect with me at www.drlatriciawilliams.com

15

RETURN

A Prophetic Call to a Holy Nation

Dr. Joyce Wilkerson

I believe God is saying to the nation: Return. Return to the altar, return to the ancient paths, return to the Blueprint that was spoken over you before time began. The invitation and warning of the Lord in this hour is for His holy nation to come out of spiritual amnesia and step back into Identity as sons, ambassadors, and Kingdom legislators.

We are in a moment of divine reset, where Heaven is confronting every form of mixture, compromise, and substitute authority that has dethroned Christ in culture and in the hearts of many. The Lord is calling His people to awaken from spiritual sleep, to shake off the dust of religion, and to be clothed again with garments of righteousness and governmental influence. He is breaking the complacency that has lulled many into silence, and He is restoring to His people the understanding that a nation is not first defined by borders or flags but by a people in covenant—people who know their God, discern their scrolls, and execute His will on Earth.

The Spirit is speaking: "I am summoning My Ecclesia back to the altar, where Identity is restored, where sound is forged, and where government is transferred." This is the hour when the threshing floor becomes the meeting place with God again. The threshing floor is where sons are separated from the slave mentality, where ambassadors are stripped of earthly agendas, where our flesh is reduced to ashes so the fire of God can burn purely. It is here where the Lord removes the reproach of Egypt—every mark of captivity, every binding Identity, every limitation of the past—so His people can possess the mountains of influence with purity.

God does not raise legislators in the palace first, but on the altar; not in positions of natural relevance first, but in places of surrender, where Heaven deposits spiritual jurisdiction, spiritual authority, and spiritual clarity.

This is the hour when prayer must be recovered—not as a ritual, but as a realm of government. Prayer is not merely communication; it is legislation. It is where verdicts are received, where decrees are executed, and where sons co-govern with the King. Heaven is calling the nation into prayer that births, prayer that governs, prayer that establishes Heaven's intention until territory reflects the will of God.

We can no longer afford to pray from the Earth up; sons must pray from Heaven down. We have been seated with Christ far above principalities, powers, and rulers of darkness, and from that seated position we legislate. This is prayer from Identity, not insecurity; prayer from Sonship, not survival. The Lord is teaching His people to hear what is spoken in the courts of Heaven so they may announce, decree, and enforce what Heaven has already sanctioned.

God is raising His Watchmen, those who stand on the walls and release Heaven's alerts. These are not fearful, silent spectators but burning voices who understand times, seasons, and territories. Watchmen are not merely prayer warriors; they are guardians of cities, prophetic sentinels who report spiritual movement, who warn, who bless, who build, and who release the sound of God into regions. Their sound is not emotional noise; it is jurisdictional authority.

God is restoring His sound to the nation—a sound rooted in Identity, purified at the altar, and empowered by the Spirit. Many have spoken without jurisdiction and therefore lacked impact, but Heaven is raising voices that carry weight because they stand in the counsel of the Lord. These are not echoes of culture; they are trumpets of Heaven.

The nation is shaking because God is dismantling false structures, ungodly systems, and demonic infrastructures that have governed the hearts and minds of generations. He is pulling down altars built to self, ambition, religion, and idolatry. He is raising pure altars again—places where His name is honored, where His fire falls, and where His presence governs.

The rebuilding of the altar is the rebuilding of the nation. Where altars are restored, Identity is restored. Where Identity is restored, authority is restored. Where authority is restored, territory responds. This is why the adversary has fought so hard to mute the voices of the saints, to break their prayer altars, and to distort their spiritual hearing—because the moment sons discover their jurisdiction, the nation shifts.

God is also speaking concerning sound, that He is distinguishing in this hour between mere prophetic voice and prophetic sound. A voice speaks, but a sound marks territory, breaks atmospheres, and establishes government. A sound communicates Identity, assignment, and spiritual location. We cannot impact a nation without Heaven's sound. Elijah conquered Baal not only by decree but because he carried Heaven's sound. The early Church was birthed by sound—*as of a rushing mighty wind* that announced Heaven's invasion.

Likewise, the nation is awaiting its next Pentecostal sound—a company of sons and daughters whose roar shakes systems, breaks chains, and aligns regions to Heaven's frequency.

This is why God is calling us to the courts of Heaven, because nations are shifted legally before they change physically. We cannot transform the land without first receiving Heaven's legal right to overturn demonic claims, generational covenants, and illegal spiritual occupants. Sons must stand in the courtroom and receive scrolls, verdicts, Blueprints, and assignments—and then release decrees into the Earth until the land comes under the jurisdiction of Heaven. The Earth responds to legality; authority flows from alignment. When sons legislate from the courts, the nation must respond.

Our impact on the nation will flow from Identity. Heaven is not looking for religious performers but for sons who know who they are—image-bearers, rulers, priests, ambassadors. Sons do not beg; they govern. Ambassadors do not take orders from earthly systems; they represent Heavenly ones. Kingdom legislators do not express opinions; they enforce law—divine law written in Heaven. The nation responds to those who legislate from the throne room, who carry Heaven's scrolls, who function in their spiritual jurisdiction.

Therefore, God is calling His people to rise as a holy nation, a royal priesthood that discerns what Heaven is saying and boldly executes it. As His people return to their Identity, rebuild altars, reclaim their roar, and occupy their seated position, we will witness divine reversals, righteous governance, spiritual reformation, and unprecedented awakening.

The nation will not be transformed by politics, personalities, or programs, but by a consecrated Ecclesia that governs from the spirit realm and manifests Heaven's rule in the natural.

This nation will bow to the Lordship of Jesus Christ when His people stand in their original mandate: to legislate Heaven on Earth, until *"the kingdoms of this world are become the kingdoms of our Lord, and of his Christ"* (Revelation 11:15), and His will is done *"in earth, as it is in heaven"* (Matthew 6:10).

As God summons His people into this hour of awakening, He is emphasizing that national transformation begins with personal consecration. Before God shifts a territory, He first shifts the hearts of those assigned to legislate within it. He is calling His people to examine the altars of their own lives, to lay down idols of comfort, compromise, and culture, and to embrace the fire of purification. From this burning place of surrender, a pure priesthood emerges—one that ministers first unto the Lord and then unto nations with clean hands and a steady voice.

A nation can only rise as high as the purity of its priesthood. Where the priesthood is defiled, the people stumble. Where the priesthood is consecrated, the people ascend into their inheritance.

God is restoring the revelation that nations are discipled, not merely influenced. Jesus did not commission us to gather believers alone; He commissioned us to disciple nations, bringing systems, cultures, and atmospheres under Heaven's influence (Matthew 28:18-19). This requires more than inspiration; it demands transformation.

Transformation begins when sons understand that their assignment is generational—that we are building altars, establishing gates, and legislating verdicts that will shape the future spiritual landscape of families, cities, and regions long after we are gone. We are laying foundation stones for future harvests. We are called to think beyond moments and minister with eternity in view.

This is why the Lord is restoring to His people an understanding of jurisdiction. You cannot legislate where you have not been authorized. Heaven assigns territories, families, cities, spheres, and industries, giving sons jurisdiction to occupy, guard, and reform them. Some are called to education, others to government, others to business, media, arts, medicine, or technology. Wherever God assigns you, you are not present as a mere participant—you are present as a governor, sent to enforce Heaven's will.

When you understand jurisdiction, your prayer becomes targeted, your decrees become precise, and your impact becomes measurable. Jurisdiction defines your sphere of influence and your sphere of responsibility.

The Lord is also emphasizing the importance of scrolls—Heavenly documents containing Identity, assignment, Blueprints, and generational purpose. Every believer carries a scroll; every family carries a scroll; every city and nation carries a scroll written by God before time. When we stand in the courts of Heaven, we receive insight into what is written. We legislate from what is written—not from emotion or assumption.

When we decree from the scroll, Heaven backs us; angels are dispatched; obstacles are removed; gates open; territory responds.

The most powerful intercession is not merely what we desire but what God has ordained.

God is dismantling the lie that spiritual authority is reserved only for clergy. In this hour, He is raising a Kingdom people who understand that every believer is a priest and a king (Revelation 1:6). Kings legislate; priests minister. The priestly and kingly dimensions must operate together. Priests minister to God, cultivating intimacy and stewarding His presence. Kings legislate, govern, and establish His decrees in the Earth.

When the priesthood is strong, the legislation of the Kingdom becomes unstoppable. When priestly devotion and kingly authority unite, the nation experiences sustained transformation.

God is also restoring spiritual intelligence to His people—the ability to perceive spiritual realities, interpret divine movement, and understand unseen dynamics shaping earthly events. Spiritual intelligence strengthens discernment, prevents compromise, protects purity, and reveals strategy.

We cannot legislate effectively without spiritual intelligence. The sons of Issachar understood the times and knew what Israel must do (1 Chronicles 12:32). In the same way, God is raising a people who understand the times and seasons of the nation, who recognize when doors open in the Spirit, and who move quickly to align Earth with Heaven before the moment passes.

The Lord is also restoring courage to His people. Kingdom legislation cannot be executed with timidity. Sons must be bold—bold to speak, bold to decree, bold to stand in the face of opposition, bold to confront systems, bold to tear down altars, bold to build new ones. The days of silent Christianity are over. The mute priesthood will not survive this hour.

God is calling forth lions—those who roar with the sound of Heaven, whose voices shake atmospheres, and whose presence announces that the Kingdom is at hand. "*The righteous are bold as a lion*" (Proverbs 28:1). This boldness is not arrogance; it is confidence in the One who has sent us.

As we step into this mandate, God is revealing the importance of community and divine alignment. No one legislates alone. Heaven operates through the corporate body. When believers unite under Heaven's counsel, they become an unstoppable legislative assembly—an Ecclesia with jurisdictional authority to bind, loose, decree, establish, and overturn. Unity multiplies authority. One can chase a thousand, but two can put ten thousand to flight (Deuteronomy 32:30).

The Lord is forming Kingdom alliances—regional and national partnerships designed to execute divine assignments at scale. These alliances are strategic, Spirit-forged, and mission-focused.

In this hour, God is also releasing a fresh wave of glory encounters—not simply emotional experiences but transformational moments. In His glory, Identity is reinforced, wounds are healed, scrolls are revealed, and assignments are clarified. Moses entered the cloud and received the Blueprint for a nation. Isaiah encountered the Lord and received a scroll that shaped his generation. Paul encountered Christ and received a commission that changed history.

Glory births assignment.

Glory empowers obedience.

Glory fuels legislation.

Without glory, there is no transformation. With glory, the impossible becomes inevitable.

All of this reveals that national transformation is not merely the result of activism; it is the fruit of spiritual government administered by a people who know their God (Daniel 11:32). The nation shifts when Heaven finds agreement in the Earth.

When sons align with Heaven, the nation must respond.

When the Ecclesia speaks from Identity, darkness loses its footing.

When priests rebuild the altar, fire falls.

When kings legislate, systems bow.

When Watchmen sound the alarm, gates open.

When ambassadors represent Christ, territories transform.

When legislators decree, the land yields.

Therefore, the call of the Spirit is urgent:

Return. Rebuild. Roar. Rule.

Take your place.

The nation is waiting for the revealing of the sons of God (Romans 8:19).

This is our moment—not to retreat, but to govern;

not to hide, but to arise;

not to echo the world, but to herald Heaven;

not to merely pray for change but to be the instruments through whom God reforms the land.

Dr. Joyce Wilkerson CDKA, is the Apostolic Leader of Restoration Global Ministry Hub in Clayton, NC.

Apostle Wilkerson is the Founder of Restoring HER Within Academy, Founder of SOAR Mentorship Program, Founder of Sister's Unlocking Apostolic spiritual empowerment movement, Restoring The Altar Prayer gathering.

She is an author, dynamic preacher, a mother and grandmother.

SECTION V: SPHERES OF IMPACT

16

GRACED TO GOVERN IN EDUCATION

A Disciple's Call to Educate and Lead with Love, Equity, Purpose, and Passion

Kara Bickhem May

Love, equity, purpose, and passion: these values are not just abstract concepts to me; they're the heartbeat of my life as an educator, a leader, and a follower of Christ - a Disciple. My journey into education has always felt like a divine appointment, even when I have wanted to abandon the calling, shaped by experiences and people who modeled what it means to lead with grace, dignity and love.

Growing up, teaching was revered in my community, a profession almost sacred. My maternal grandfather, a pastor to many and my childhood hero, embodied the essence of what it means to live a life of service. He came from humble beginnings in Yazoo City, Mississippi, leaving behind his father's plantation and a life of familiarity to earnestly and ardently follow God's call to the Ministry. I used to always say that Grandpapa ("Daddy" as I grew to call him) was the closest to perfect a human could ever be, for he was a man of immense love and compassion, and his faith permeated every aspect of his life. He was the kind of person who would give without hesitation, who listened without judgement and prayed for people - whether the person expressed the need of such behavior or not, who hosted Dr. King in his home, and who fought tirelessly for social justice. To me, he was a living example of Christ's love in action. Was he *actually* perfect? Of course not, but he had his love wiring down-pat.

LOVE

It was Grandpapa who first inspired me to lead with love. His influence is woven into my DNA as both a human and an educator. He - and other education-involved family members - taught me that teaching isn't just about imparting knowledge; it's about seeing the full humanity in each child, nurturing their God-given potential, and loving them as Christ loves us. This is not always easy; in fact, it is often difficult - very difficult. But those life lessons have stayed with me, blooming into a full-fledged philosophy and, dare I say, indignation about how children should be treated - shaping how I approach my work, my students, and even myself.

I vividly remember my early years of teaching. I was young, eager, a bit overconfident and soon overwhelmed by the weight of the responsibility. I walked into that classroom determined to make a difference, but I quickly realized that it wasn't, by any means, just about good intentions, lesson plans and grades. One student, in particular, deeply challenged the rules that I held as my non-contextual "truth." She was withdrawn, angry, and had already been written off by many as a lost cause. I struggled to reach her until one day, I remembered Grandpapa's words: "*If you don't love people, Kara - truly love them - they won't hear you.*" Wow.

So, I began to *love* on her - not in a surface-level, clichéd way, but deeply and intentionally. I showed up for her, hosted her after school for tutoring-turned relationship building, listened to her stories, and quickly saw her as more than her behavior. Over time, that intentional love - that heart shift - broke down barriers that she had erected as a small child due to hurt, trauma and loss. She began to trust me, and eventually, she started to thrive. Moreover, the softening of her walls demonstrated for many other students that they were safe to do the same. That experience cemented my belief that love is the foundation of effective teaching, but it also taught me something more profound: that grace is essential in education - and that I was *graced* to show it.

Grace, in this context, means creating space for students to fail, grow, and be redeemed. It means extending patience when progress feels slow and choosing forgiveness when mistakes are made - after all: we *all* make mistakes. Grace allows us to see beyond immediate challenges and envision the potential that God has placed within every child. Without grace, love becomes conditional, equity becomes hollow, and purpose and passion lose their grounding. And, be it literally or figuratively, people die empty and alone.

Leadership in education also requires grace. As leaders, we are called to shepherd not only our students but also our fellow educators and communities. Effective leadership demands discernment, humility, and a deep commitment to fostering environments where everyone feels valued and supported. Grace empowers us to navigate conflicts with wisdom, to mentor others with patience, and to remain steadfast in our vision - even when obstacles arise. A quick learning for me as I stepped into more and more leadership roles was that if my expectation was that an adult lend children even a portion of the grace I had learned to extend, how dare I *not* extend the grace to them - the adults - as well. The elevation of Romans 3:23 (NLT) grew in my heart and echoed in my spirit: *"For everyone has sinned; we all fall short of God's glorious standard."* Boundaries and professionalism notwithstanding, we *all* need the grace that our great God extends, regardless of age, status, gender or any other societally-defining construct.

EQUITY

Yes, love is amazing - a gift from God himself, but love should be a baseline expectation for practice in a field in which we are entrusted with the hearts and futures of young people. That said, my journey has also taught me the critical importance of equity. I have had the privilege of serving in many educational spaces where dreams abound but equity does not. Connecting with organizations to address the systemic barriers our students face is critical, but so is understanding that equity and equality are not the same. With equality, we give and treat all the same, regardless of need, background or circumstances. Equity, to me, is about more than just leveling the playing field; it's about understanding and addressing each student's unique needs. It's about creating pathways for them to reach their full potential, even when the world has placed obstacles in their way - when society has written them an uncashable check for the future they envision.

I think back to a young man at the creative arts school of which I was the founding principal who had incredible artistic talent but lacked confidence and adequate life support. He reminded me of so many students with whom I had come in contact: full of dreams and bright ideas but unsure of how to make them a reality; unsure of how his vision for his life could ever be realized. By providing him with tangible resources, mentorship, and a space to express himself in healthy, affirming ways, we saw him blossom, year over year. Via our efforts, his family saw a different version of him and ultimately a different framework for what their corporate future could look like. *That* is the power of equity: it's transformative, not just for students but for entire communities. And yet, equity work is only sustainable when it is approached with grace. True grace allows us to meet each student where they are, without judgment or preconceived notions, and to walk alongside them as they navigate their journeys - not in judgement but in partnership, with reflective hearts on the sacrifice Christ made for us *constantly* running in the background of our increasingly more digitized brains and hearts.

Leading through the equity of it all, it is critical to remember that grace - like love - is not passive; it is active and requires intentionality. It calls us to see beyond data points and test scores, past the eyes and into the soul of each child - even when they do not understand what we are doing or why. The very memory of applied grace itself provides a sense of spiritual "checks and balances." It is the bridge between the ideal and the reality, reminding us that progress is usually incremental and often invisible, but it is there, like the steady rhythm of a heartbeat or the undercurrent of the ocean. Our reflection of grace challenges us to stay present, to celebrate growth even when it feels small, and to trust in the transformative power of consistent, intentional love paired with truly equitable practices.

PURPOSE AND PASSION

I am an artist. Family lore dictates that I sang before I even spoke, often humming along with whatever music was playing around me: church hymns, Marvin Gaye, The Temptations, The Thompson Community Singers...all of it! My first church solo was "Goin' Up Yonder" by the incomparable Tremaine Hawkins. Picture a five- or six-year-old Jiffy peanut butter-colored girl with pigtails standing in front of the church, baby-belting the lyrics, *"If you wanna knoooooww...wh-ere I am goiiiiiiinnng... wh-ere I am goiiiiiiing...sooooonnnn...I'm goin' up 'a Yahhhnder..."* It was a sight, as evidenced by pictures I have seen: eyes squinted, mouth wide open, heart open wider - I was very clearly feeling that thing! This part of my being would continue to grow, and since that time, my passion for the arts has been a driving force in my life. As time progressed, I would branch off into writing, acting, and other forms of self-expression, and the arts would be where I'd find joy and purpose, a gift I believe God placed in me to share with others. Providing arts opportunities for students has allowed me to connect with them in profound ways, helping them to explore their own creativity and discover who they are via their soul's very wiring. It has also helped me to more deeply connect with who I am, building more congruous alignment with God as THE Creator, and me, made in His image, as a creative.

There's a particular God Moment that happens when purpose and passion intersect - it's often where I feel most aligned with His Will, where my work becomes a tangible act of worship. Yet, this intersection of purpose and passion also requires grace. It's easy to become frustrated or burned out when challenges arise, but grace reminds us to rest in God's strength rather than our own. His strength is sufficient; ours is not. His grace is sufficient; ours, on the other hand, is not (2 Corinthians 12:9). Grace calls us to persevere, to find joy in small victories, and to trust that our labor is not in vain. Although there are times when I, in my humanity, miss grace's call, I am constantly grateful for - humbled and amazed by - the countless stories of transformation I've witnessed over my many years in education - both in my students and in myself. Each moment brings new tests, but also new chances to grow and serve. Navigating an educational career requires more than just expertise; it demands a committed, fervent posture of faith, love, humility, and grace. Teaching - and school leadership for that matter - are not simply careers. They are life-walks that evolve over time, shaped by the lessons we learn and the grace we extend to others *and* ourselves.

Scripture continually serves to ground me in this work. My alignment *and* effectiveness depend on my connection to God and the truths that are revealed and reinforced in His Word. For example, Proverbs 22:6 reminds us, "*Train up a child in the way he should go; even when he is old he will not depart from it.*" This verse underscores the sacred duty - the spiritual obligation - we hold as believer-educators and believer-leaders to guide our students on their designated paths of purpose. Micah 6:8 teaches us, *"He has shown you, O mortal, what is good. And what does the Lord require of you? To act justly and to love mercy and to walk humbly with your God."* These words admonish me to pursue equity and justice with grace and humility. And for times when I am feeling less than - or I am *not quite* seeing the "greater than" in my students, colleagues and families, Ephesians 2:10 proclaims, *"For we are God's handiwork, created in Christ Jesus to do good works, which God prepared in advance for us to do."* This truth reminds me that our work in education is part of His divine plan - and that we ALL have a role to play in order to see His Kingdom come in the earth.

I have found that true resilience in this work comes from staying rooted in my purpose and passion, continually seeking God's guidance to travel through the various complexities and nuances of education and its presenting landscape. Galatians 6:9 reminds me, *"Let us not grow weary in doing good, for at the proper time we will reap a harvest if we do not give up."* It is this promise that sustains me - even on days when I want to check out completely. Praise God for His continued work in me as I seek to work for Him!

To my fellow educators and leaders, particularly those seeking to represent Christ in all that you do: I encourage you to find your own stories, to remember the moments that shaped you and the people who inspired you. Let those stories fuel your passion and guide your purpose. Lean into love, strive for equity, and embrace the grace that God has given you to govern in this sacred work. In Ed Space, we are often called to pour out endlessly, but grace also teaches us the necessity of replenishment - in the Natural as well as in the Spirit Realm, there is no service from an empty vessel. It is through our regular communication with The Father, personal reflection, wellness practices and community connection that we find the strength to continue. Our universal need for His matchless grace reminds us that we are not alone in this work, that the same God who calls us to this mission truly does equip us for every challenge, whether we see it or not. As author Lisa Delpit wrote in her book *Other People's Children: Cultural Conflict in the Classroom*, "I pray for all of us the strength to teach our children what they must learn, and the humility and wisdom to learn from them so that we might teach better." And as the Apostle Paul wrote in his letter to the church in Colossae, *"Whatever you do, work heartily, as for the Lord and not for men"* (Colossians 3:23). Our students deserve nothing less, and the future depends on the grace that we are blessed to give.

Kara Bickhem May is an educator, vocalist, and ministry leader whose **over three decades** of service are rooted in faith and a calling to uplift others through love. As Executive Director of Arts & Partnerships at Art In Motion and an Educational Partner with Free to Dream, she strengthens communities and expands creative opportunity with intention and care. Kara helps people find their voice, walk in purpose, and pursue the God-shaped dreams placed within them.

17
THE LEGACY OF A GIVING HEART

Posturing Our Hearts for Generations to Come

Donna Rena Lowry

If there is one legacy I desire to leave for this generation and for the generations that follow it is the legacy of giving: a heart postured toward generosity, sensitivity to the Holy Spirit, and obedience when God whispers, "Give."

People often say, "It's easy for you to give because you have abundance," and in a way, they're right. A millionaire can give freely without fearing lack. But what we often forget is that abundance is not ownership. Wealth, resources, opportunities do not belong to us. They belong to God, who entrusts them to us for purpose.

The measure of giving isn't found in someone's bank account.

It's found in a heart that recognizes God as the true source of all things.

Abundance did not teach me to give.

God taught me to give long before I ever held abundance.

My heart was postured early **in the seasons of lack, not in the seasons of overflow.**

When Every Penny Mattered

I remember pulling up to the gas station with exact change in my hand, terrified that if the pump went one penny over, I wouldn't be able to pay. I held that pump with the same caution someone might handle something fragile and priceless. At that time in my life, every cent mattered.

When my husband and I first married, we counted loose change for lunch money. We opened empty cabinets and prayed for meals yet God provided each time. A friend would drop off dinner without knowing our needs. Someone would invite us over at the exact moment we had nothing left.

We lived humbly not out of despair, but out of reverence for the God who placed every blessing into our hands.

During one of those seasons, I prayed,

"Lord, if You ever bless me with abundance, I will give in abundance."

And God responded with a question that changed my life:

"What are you doing with what you have now?"

Giving Is Not Measured by the Amount

Scripture tells of the widow's mite (Mark 12:41–44). Her offering looked small, but Heaven valued it because it cost her something.

God reminded me that giving is not measured by:

- the amount
- the public recognition
- or the applause

Giving is measured by **sacrifice**, **motive**, and **posture of heart**.

So, I began giving in small places. Not for repayment. Not for validation. Simply because God was forming a cheerful, obedient giver in me.

"God loves a cheerful giver." — 2 Corinthians 9:7

"Whatever a man sows, that shall he also reap." — Galatians 6:7

Learning Not to Expect from People

Growing up, my idea of giving was simple:

If you give to me, I give to you; if you don't, you're off my list.

My father used to say, "Rena, God loves a cheerful giver, you shouldn't give with expectation to receive" but I didn't understand it then. It wasn't until adulthood and spiritual maturity that I learned:

True giving asks nothing in return.

Many people struggle with giving because they give with expectations. Expectations often lead to disappointment.

A woman once told me she felt hurt that people she considered "close friends" never checked on her during a time of grief. She appreciated the meals I brought, but was disappointed in others.

God opened a door for me to gently ask,

"Was your expectation in people supplying your need—or God?"

She paused, realizing she had expected man to do what only God promises.

"It is better to trust in the Lord than to put confidence in man." — Psalm 118:8

"I have never seen the righteous forsaken nor his seed begging bread." — Psalm 37:25

Later she called to say, "God supplied every meal... just through different people than I expected."

And in that revelation, her heart healed.

The $20 That Changed Everything

Extraordinary Provision in an Ordinary Place

One of the most defining moments of my life happened in Bo's Grocery Store in Pembroke during the early years of our marriage—when faith carried us further than finances ever could.

I walked in with just enough money for a few groceries, deodorant and hairspray. Essentials only. As I passed the frozen aisle, I saw my favorite ice cream—Breyers Butter Pecan—on sale. I sighed and pushed my cart forward. After gathering the food essentials and calculating the cost I had enough money left to purchase hairspray or deodorant, but not both. I remember thinking, "I need to smell good and I need to have my hair in place".

In my heart I whispered, Lord, if only I had a few extra dollars...

An elderly woman approached me with handmade wooden spoons and asked if I'd like to buy one. I explained that I couldn't afford to purchase anything beyond the necessities.

She didn't walk away.

Instead, she stayed.

She talked about the Lord with a tenderness that filled the aisle.

Then she said, "May I pray with you?"

Right there in the middle of the grocery store we bowed our heads.

When the prayer ended, she squeezed my hand... and slipped something into my palm that felt like paper.

When I opened my hand it was a $20 bill.

Before I could look up, she was gone.

The Holy Spirit whispered:

"Now you have enough."

Enough for deodorant.

Enough for hairspray.

Enough for ice cream.

I cried all the way to checkout. When I got home, Charles came outside asking if something was wrong. Through tears I said:

"Nothing is wrong. We've been blessed."

That night we praised the Lord. And I prayed:

"God, if You ever allow me to bless someone the way she blessed me, I will be obedient expecting nothing in return."

The Journey of Giving Continues

Years later, after becoming a nurse, I held my first paycheck. I paid my tithes and offerings, and then God brought that woman back to my memory.

That day, I folded a $20 bill and placed it in my wallet.

"God, anytime You speak to me to "Give" this $20 bill any place, any moment I will give."

In a grocery store. Mall. Church. Vacation.

Anywhere.

Eventually the $20 bill became a $50 bill.

Then a $100 bill.

To this day, I keep a $100 bill tucked in my wallet not for me, but for God to use.

God taught me that giving is not about:

- convenience,
- judging who "looks" like they need it,
- or receiving credit.

It's about obedience.

> "Let the elders that rule well be counted worthy of double honor." — 1 Timothy 5:17

Generosity creates a culture—a rhythm—a lifestyle.

The enemy fights generosity because he understands the power behind a giving heart. But when we keep giving, something beautiful grows in us:

Honor.

Spiritual Maturity.

Compassion.

Joy.

It all started with a need, a woman I never met again, and a $20 bill.

The Legacy I Want To Leave

Intentional giving shapes the heart.
It breaks selfishness.
It builds unity.
It produces spiritual maturity.
It reinforces honor.

Giving is not about money.
It is about posture.
It is about sensitivity to God.
It is about obedience without hesitation.
It is about being a vessel God can trust.

It is about sowing without ever expecting something back from man—because God alone is our source.

Generosity is not accidental.
It is taught.
It is modeled.
It is chosen.
It is lived.

If there is anything, I want this generation and those after me to remember, it is this:

> **May they say…**
>
> **"She taught us how to give.**
>
> **She taught us how to trust God.**
>
> **She taught us how to posture our hearts."**
>
> That is the legacy I leave behind.

Kingdom-preneur Donna Rena Lowry, a visionary entrepreneur and philanthropist, is the founder and CEO of Caring Touch Home and Behavioral Healthcare. With over 20 years of leadership, a U.S. patent, and numerous accolades, she blends innovation, ministry, and service, empowering her community and exemplifying excellence in both business and faith-driven initiatives. Donna is married to Charles Lowry, and together they have a daughter, Alexis.

18

YOUR FUNDAMENTAL LEGAL RIGHT TO ABIDE IN THE BRAND NAME

Sharlina Mack

A Message to Caregivers, Parents, Government, Community, Church, and Children

God has granted humankind free will—a fundamental liberty He will not violate. This liberty echoes earthly constitutions but supersedes them in authority and purpose. The original battle—the war in Heaven—now plays out on Earth. The conflict between Lucifer and the angels who fell with him continues as the Secret Counsel of Satan strives to divert people from receiving and walking in the Secret Counsel of the Lord.

The good news is this: When we receive Jesus Christ as Lord and Savior, a Brand is revealed—the Name above every name—and we are born again into a new family with trust accounts, benefits, and a mandate (John 1:12; Ephesians 1:3-14). We become new creatures (2 Corinthians 5:17), adopted as sons and daughters (Romans 8:15), receiving access to a New Brand Name—our Identity in Christ.

> *"If ye abide in me, and my words abide in you, ye shall ask what ye will, and it shall be done unto you"* (John 15:7).

This is more than business, trademarks, or corporate status. This Brand is eternal, outlasting Heaven and Earth. *"The word of our God shall stand for ever"* (Isaiah 40:8) The Brand does not merely cover us; it recreates us. It does not grant partial shares; it calls us to full reward—thirty, sixty, and a hundredfold—by obedience (Mark 4:20; 1 Samuel 15:22).

From Government Name to Kingdom Name

In the natural, you bear a legal or "government" name. In the Spirit, you receive a Kingdom Name, a seal of Identity and assignment. This name-change is covenantal. You are translated from the mark of the beast—a system of flesh, fear, and false worship—into the mark of the Spirit, the seal of the Holy Ghost (Revelation 13; Ephesians 1:13-14). Limits recede. Boundary lines expand. You are a unique brand—His workmanship, created in Christ Jesus unto good works (Ephesians 2:10).

The Brand Name is within you because Christ in you is the hope of glory (Colossians 1:27). As you abide in Him, He abides in you (John 15). Then your life becomes a visible testimony, compelling others to glorify your Father (Matthew 5:16).

> *"And whatsoever ye do in word or deed, do all in the name of the Lord Jesus"* (Colossians 3:17).

The Prophetic Call: Learn Your Brand

Prophetic Voice: *"I am yours and you are Mine, saith the Lord. I will teach you your brand—who you are and whose you are—so that when you are tempted, you will not deny Me. Truth and Life are the brand beneath your surface; not carnal, but spiritual. Abide in Me, and I will grant you access—24/7—by My Word and Spirit. I have anointed and appointed you* (Jeremiah 1:5) *to teach, train, and make disciples* (Matthew 28:19-20). *As My Bride, abide in covenant, and I will pour out My Spirit upon all flesh."*

This is the Brand life: Mark 16 signs following believers (Mark 16:17-18), gifts given for the common good (1 Corinthians 12), and daily communion with God who orders our steps.

Mandated to Return Daily

You were born into a world of sin (Psalm 51:5; Romans 3:23), yet you carry a Kingdom brand and mandate. Obstacles will appear, but you are ordained to trample them (Luke 10:19). Your safety is in daily returning to the Lord—receiving His instruction, obeying His voice, and walking in His promises. Deuteronomy 28 outlines the blessings of hearing and obeying: blessed in your coming in and going out; provision that you did not build; protection that you did not earn but Christ purchased.

Your travel, reach, and assignments will carry purpose—to teach, train, equip, and compel others to return to God (Luke 14:23). You are designed to align. You are created on purpose, for purpose, and with purpose (Ephesians 2:10). You will help others discover their brand beneath the surface and walk as a people blessed of the Lord (Genesis 12:2-3).

> *"For I know the thoughts that I think toward you, saith the Lord ... to give you an expected end"* (Jeremiah 29:11).

The School of the Holy Spirit

Upon new birth, you are granted entrance into the School of the Holy Spirit—not a carnal academy but a Kingdom formation. Here you are taught, trained, disciplined, loved, structured, organized, and equipped for the Lord's bidding (John 14:26). Your mandate and mantle are revealed. Like a soldier wears armor, you are to wear your mantle and walk in your mandate (Ephesians 6:10-18).

> *"For the weapons of our warfare are not carnal, but mighty through God to the pulling down of strong holds"* (2 Corinthians 10:4).

David's slingshot looked ordinary, but the true weapon was his faith and heart (1 Samuel 17). In this School, faith will be tested (1 Peter 1:7). You will be taught to return everything to God—plans, wins, losses—and to bless the Lord at all times (Psalm 34:1). Your praise is trust in His character before the outcome appears (Hebrews 11:6).

This training is progressive: from *nepios* (infant) to *paidion/teknon* (child/disciple), to *huios* (mature son), toward *teleios* (maturity/wholeness). You grow by abiding in Christ (John 15), walking in the Spirit (Galatians 5:16-25), and resisting the flesh and its appetites.

The Secret Counsel: Two Tables, One Choice

There are two counsels at work:

- The Secret Counsel of the Lord (Psalm 25:14; Amos 3:7), where wisdom, holiness, and obedience govern the heart.
- The Secret Counsel of Satan, an imitation school discipling through witchcraft, rebellion, and lies.

Each human must choose. *"Choose you this day whom ye will serve"* (Joshua 24:15). God dignifies your choice, but your choices determine your jurisdiction—blessing or bondage. When believers walk in the flesh, they forfeit the jurisdictional blessings of the Kingdom and become vulnerable to deception. But we overcome—*"by the blood of the Lamb, and by the word of [our] testimony"* (Revelation 12:11).

Satan tempts to shift Identity, to sell "an easier way," to offer a back door to blessing without obedience (Genesis 3; Matthew 4:1-11). But Christ is the Way, the Truth, and the Life (John 14:6). The Father uses even testing to mature you. Therefore, crucify the flesh (Galatians 5:24), walk in the Spirit, and let patience have her perfect work (James 1:2-4).

The Parental, Ecclesial, and Civic Mandate

Training belongs not only to households but also to church and community, and it is observed—whether consciously or not—by governments, whose systems are shaped by the beliefs of the humans who lead them. While earthly governments often house and treat symptoms, Christ's Church is commissioned to disciple nations (Matthew 28:19-20), train the young (Proverbs 22:6), and mature saints for the work of ministry (Ephesians 4:11-16).

Children and parents perish *"for lack of knowledge"* (Hosea 4:6). But the Holy Spirit fills the gaps—healing traumas, renewing minds, and restoring years *"that the locust hath eaten"* (Joel 2:25). In Christ, we are given power to tread on serpents and scorpions and over all the power of the enemy (Luke 10:19). We are assigned legal jurisdiction to set things in order (Titus 1:5).

Therefore, make a choice: faith or fear, surrender or self-reliance. God has not called us to manage image; He has called us to govern Identity—by grace.

Abiding Guarantees the Expected End

> *"Being confident of this very thing, that he which hath begun a good work in you will perform it . . . "* (Philippians 1:6).

The Father's commands are not control; they are covenant safety. Obedience forms guardrails that usher you into your expected end. Satan may desire to sift, but Christ has prayed for your faith (Luke 22:31-32). Rise, return, and abide.

If parents are absent or support systems thin, the Holy Ghost Himself is your Teacher and Comforter (John 14:26; 16:13). Kingdom training is not merely educate–medicate–diagnose; it is disciple–equip–deploy. We help children and adults discover gifts, walk in purpose, and align to God's plan (Jeremiah 29:11). The Spirit supplies what was missing and strengthens what remains.

Governance, Culture, and the Wars of Belief

Nations legislate from belief—spoken or hidden. This is why governmental battles so often mirror spiritual ones. But *"the battle is the Lord's"* (1 Samuel 17:47). Our part is to be led by the Spirit; *"for as many as are led by the Spirit of God, they are the sons of God"* (Romans 8:14, KJV). Humans are free to choose, but true choice requires truth (John 8:32). Therefore, we teach, we train, we testify, and we govern—in love.

> *"And there are also many other things which Jesus did . . . if they should be written every one, I suppose that even the world itself could not contain the books . . . "* (John 21:25).

You are a living epistle (2 Corinthians 3:2-3). Leave a record that points others home.

Walking Out the Brand

1. Receive the Brand – Confess Jesus as Lord; receive adoption, sealing, and new creation Identity (Romans 10:9-10; Ephesians 1:13-14; 2 Corinthians 5:17).
2. Abide Daily – Word and prayer as your first jurisdiction (John 15:4-7).
3. Train Continually – Submit to the School of the Holy Spirit; grow from infant faith to mature sonship.
4. Guard the Gates – Refuse counterfeit counsel; discern spirits; test doctrines (1 John 4:1).
5. Govern by Love and Truth – Obedience over optics; holiness over hype (John 14:15; 1 Samuel 15:22).
6. Disciple Others – Teach children, strengthen families, equip saints, and serve the city (Proverbs 22:6; Ephesians 4:12; Matthew 28:19-20).
7. Expect Full Reward – Believe for thirty, sixty, and a hundredfold as you obey (Mark 4:20).

Declarations (Pray These)

- I choose the Secret Counsel of the Lord; I renounce the counsel of darkness.
- I receive my New Brand Name in Christ and walk as a new creation.
- I abide in the Word; the Word abides in me; my prayers are aligned and answered.

- I am trained by the School of the Holy Spirit and armed for righteous governance.
- By the blood of the Lamb and the word of my testimony, I overcome.
- My household is discipled; our gates are guarded; our destiny is governed by grace.
- I expect the full reward of obedience—thirty, sixty, and a hundredfold.

> "*But grow in grace, and in the knowledge of our Lord and Saviour Jesus Christ*" (2 Peter 3:18).

To impact a generation, we must govern Identity at its root—in Christ. We restore the honor of choice by teaching truth, and we restore the power of governance by training hearts to abide. Parents, pastors, teachers, public servants, and culture-makers: This is our collective mandate. Raise brands, not merely names. Form sons and daughters who can discern counsel, carry mantles, and advance the Kingdom with integrity.

Grace to govern is not control—it is covenant alignment. It is the holy stewardship of people's God-given liberty so they can freely choose the Lord's counsel and flourish. As we abide in the Brand Name—JESUS—our homes, churches, and cities will witness what only God can do: families restored, systems reformed, and nations discipled.

> "*Now unto him that is able to do exceeding abundantly above all that we ask or think … Unto him be glory in the church by Christ Jesus throughout all ages, world without end. Amen*" (Ephesians 3:20-21).

Apostle Sharlina Pye Mack, J.D., a licensed and ordained minister, attorney, mediator, coach and teacher. She has coached youth and been actively involved in ministry for over 30 years. She is mandated to teach others how to Grow to Walk together and begin to Work to Gather.

19

GOVERNANCE BY WAY OF PRESENCE

Psalmist Raine

One solemn day, I was driving in the car when I had a moment that was dangerous in every sense of the word. I was driving and yet not present. I don't even remember how I got to my destination. Have you had one of those moments?

Although this was super dangerous, it was also extremely informative. It resembled one of those moments written in the Bible where someone had an encounter with the Lord or was taken up in a vision. The intel I received struck my heart in such an intense way. In just a matter of minutes, I quickly understood the brokenness founded in the doctrine of the Kingdom that has traveled throughout the body of Christ across multiple decades.

The partial understanding of God's heart concerning the Kingdom has truly impacted the reality and mindset of the present generation. It can be extremely costly to transfer partial doctrine and revelation to an advancing generation coming behind. The rising generation will run with their perverse interpretation as a reflection of the heart of God, and the present generation will have to continue to dig up and relay a clearer foundation. We have seen it so many times before. As a result of this, the advancement of the Kingdom has become more stagnant than progressive, and the dissonance between the truth and power of the Kingdom as a solution to our world is ever increasing.

Now, back to the encounter at hand. It grieved my heart to see that the idea of Kingdom had only boiled down to the understanding of dominance instead of transformation, and it has happened all in the name of the Lord. Instead of industries and atmospheres being transformed for God's glory and empowered for God's work, I saw people being undermined and subdued. What a grief?!? Then, the Lord spoke to my heart His intentions. The aspect of the Kingdom that focused on dominion and authority was not about ruling over others. It was about our stewardship over the conditions of this realm we called Earth. Then, He began to reveal how our responsibility of stewardship was about guarding the Glory of God in every active sphere. Genesis 2:15 states, "... *And the Lord God took the man, and put him into the garden of Eden to dress it and to keep it.*"

The command of the Lord to the man was the same instruction of responsibility given to us. In essence, where I place you, tend to it, guard it, and maintain it. However, we have gotten far away from this work. We have taken the posture that this is not our responsibility and that it wasn't our fault. Making statements in our hearts and minds like, "We didn't start it; we are not responsible for it." This thought process has typically been the response that we have taken about global, regional, and maybe even local matters; but the impact of spheres and fields that produce the fruit of transformation begins right within us, not outside of us. We are the small pebble of change that has a dynamic ripple effect on the world around us.

Needless to say, the reality of dominion that reflects the heart of God requires that we take our place of guardianship and steward our placement well. This is what truly defines and reflects God's heart around dominion. Psalm 24:1-2 states, "*The earth is the Lord's, and the fulness thereof; the world, and they that dwell therein. For He hath founded it upon the seas, and established it upon the floods.*" This atmosphere we have been placed in is called Earth. The Lord founded it and established it. He placed us here and gave us the task of taking care of this same space He has founded and established. What a role of trust! We have been entrusted by God to take care of and protect this space He has invested in.

By its official definition, to steward means to look after, and a guardian is one who protects. The function of guardianship adds the authority given to a person to protect that which has been given to him. This should give us a picture of what our dominion should really look like. The authority we have has been given to us by the Lord. We, the ones given the authority, have been placed here to look after this place called Earth and protect it.

The harsh reality of this responsibility is that it has been given to all men, and we have to make the choice of what influence we will exercise our authority from. This truth concerning our dominion has not been passed down through generations. It has not been shared with our families. It has not been a reminder for us as God's people (Deuteronomy 6:6-11). As a result, we have not appropriately prepared our environment and even our children for what they must pass down to future generations.

As I have journeyed through life, I have realized that the only true way to steward and guard this realm that we have been placed in is to do so in alignment with the One who has founded and established it. The only way to do so is to be in a relationship with and to walk through life in close proximity to the One who has called and established this place. We can only do so through engagement and holy communion with the Lord.

We have been talking about the time where the creation has been moaning and groaning for the sons of God to be revealed (Romans 8:22). Sons are birthed through presence. We, as the sons of God, are revived through receiving the Lord Jesus Christ as our Savior and then embracing a personal transformation that reflects the Glory of God. The Lord transforms us by changing the way we think (Romans 12:2). The evidence and fruit of this change is so powerful that it has impacted the lives of God's people for years. This same shift in our mind impacts our actions and decision-making, and the more we commune with God, the more we begin to reflect God and His ways in everything that we do. Honestly, this is the heart of God for us. This should be our norm. We have made God and His ways more difficult than He planned for it to be.

If you can imagine, the more we adopt this as a norm in our lives, the more impact we will make in our lifetime and set the stage for the impact beyond our life's span. This is the time and season we are in. It is a new era of impact. It's beyond mere words; it is action; it is power (1 Corinthians 4:20). It is evident in how we think. It is expressed through the wisdom we operate in, which flows from God. This is that same grace that causes the hope of His glory to shine brightly for all who live in darkness, that they may find their way to Him. This is that same hope, victory, and light shined amongst Israel and Judah during David's tenure as king. The fruit and evidence of his governance was transferred to his son Solomon for roughly twenty years. David and Solomon were very strong examples of presence-based governance that released generational impact for God's people for approximately sixty years.

David spent his forty-year reign following the plan and Blueprint God had established throughout his tenure. When he first became king, his first mission was for the presence of God to return. It had been known across nations that wherever the Ark (the presence of God) was, that's where victory would reside. Israel had lost the Ark in war. This moment was devastating for Israel, as it was a part of the judgment due to the mismanagement of the presence of the Lord from the priesthood (Eli's lineage: 1 Samuel 4).

Many may not connect the dots, but when we mismanage or become too familiar with the Holy presence of God, we run the risk of losing what is the marker of our difference in the Earth. It was devastating for the Holy Presence of God to be with a nation who carried no knowledge or history with God and His presence. The Philistines, the ones who captured the Ark, thought it was a token of victory. Israel knew it was the lifeline of God's people, just as we know that the presence of God in our lives is life to us, and it produces life around us.

David, as noted by God as the one who had His heart, planned the recapturing of the Ark as his first mission as king. His action noted more than just a mission, but it set a priority in place that revealed the necessity of presence for governance. David established the entire structure of presence-based governance through the reorganizing of the priesthood, the entire nation of Israel, and their function. This is the first time we see the model of continual daily worship vs. annual festivals and moments of worship. We see priests and Levites in various functions, round the clock, pursuing the heart of God and functioning in different spheres from that place. When the king requested to know what the Lord was saying, an answer was given by those who pursued the presence of the Lord, and that helped determine the king's next moves (1 Chronicles 24-26). Even in the midst of battle, David moved only after seeking the Lord's heart. This was a normal pattern of governance, and it was successful. King David rarely moved on behalf of the nation in any manner without receiving instructions from the Lord. The result/fruit of this model was victory. David did not win wars or territories, uniting God's people, simply because he was strong. David was wise enough to know that he could not successfully govern this space without God. The foundation he laid throughout his tenure set his son Solomon up for success without having to labor hard for it. This is a true model of generational impact.

David gave his son Solomon a charge to keep for his tenure of rulership in 1 Kings 2.

> *"Now the days of David drew nigh that he should die; and he charged Solomon his son, saying: 'I go the way of all the earth: be thou strong therefore, and shew thyself a man; And keep the charge of the Lord thy God, to walk in his ways, to keep his statutes, and his commandments, and his judgments, and his testimonies, as it is written in the law of Moses, that thou mayest prosper in all that thou doest, and whithersoever thou turnest thyself: That the Lord may continue his word which he spake concerning me, saying, If thy children take heed to their way, to walk before me in truth with all their heart and with all their soul, there shall not fail thee (said he) a man on the throne of Israel."*

This place of dominion and governance was always supposed to be rooted and built on the foundation of fellowship with God. The only way for your ways to be empowered to walk in His way is through strong fellowship with God. You must be determined to keep your heart there. If you do so, what flows out of your governance in every sphere God places you in shall be righteous according to the One who has founded and established it.

As we see through David and Solomon's tenure as kings, the generational establishment of righteous governance can truly shift our world as we know and have seen it. On the flip side, just as Solomon eventually compromised, we can also see that there can be destructive implications generationally if we are swayed to function in unrighteousness. However, for the sake of this context, the example between David and Solomon demonstrated that this is not a governance fueled by prejudices and preferences. It is not a governance established through the eyes of envy and greed. This is a governance that reflects what God truly wants to establish. The truth of the matter is, you can only receive this intimate level of intel and revelation through your time of communion in the presence of the Lord. It cannot be duplicated, and you cannot operate as a showman in this. It is revealed through your actions and decisions on the Earth. You will find that the presence of the Lord needs to be the driving force and the fuel for everything you do, if you wish to function in righteous stewardship as He desires.

The level of governance that we should be functioning in is not something that is solely maintained within our own spheres or places of familiarity. It is something that should be spread abroad. This is the heart of the great commission in Matthew 28:18-20. So, the impact of our presence-based governance should be evident in the expansion of the Kingdom. Expansion happens through mobilization; that's why the commission was to "Go." In order for mobilization to take place in any vehicle, you need fuel. Fuel may be through a liquid, such as gasoline, or a current, such as electricity. In our case, the Holy Spirit is the living water (liquid) and the power (current) that is necessary for the mobilization of the Kingdom. This is a vital part of the reason why Jesus charged the Apostles not to go until the Holy Spirit had baptized them with power (Acts 1: 4-8). The Holy Spirit, the gift and evidence of God's presence, is the fuel for our impact. We can only mobilize in governance through time, spheres, and spaces through the power of His Spirit. His presence gives you access to HIS power, which fuels every ability you carry both naturally and supernaturally. These truths through Scripture confirm the influence and power of God's presence in our lives.

First, you need to know with confidence that the presence of the Lord empowers you with grace to accomplish everything He places in your heart to do, in accordance with the measure of Christ's gift (Ephesians 4:7).

Second, it is the enabling power of His presence that allows you to do all things through Christ (Philippians 4:13).

Last, he grants you sustaining and enduring power by His presence. He gives you strength and the ability to endure (Isaiah 40:29-31).

The presence of God, the gift of His Holy Spirit, is your fuel to rule and reign in righteousness. Just like David moved in his governance, reassured and settled that there is no other way, may it be the same for you. For God's way is the only way that produces everlasting fruit and eternal impact. This is our goal.

> *"If ye abide in me, and my words abide in you, ye shall ask what ye will, and it shall be done unto you. Herein is my Father glorified, that ye bear much fruit; so shall ye be my disciples … Ye have not chosen me, but I have chosen you, and ordained you, that ye should go and bring forth fruit, and that your fruit should remain: that whatsoever ye shall ask of the Father in my name, he may give it to you"* (John 15: 7-8, 16).

Jesus commands us to abide and shares with us the impact both with God, our Father, and within our lives. That impact is simply God glorified, fruit produced. However, it is not fruit that withers away. Jesus says it is fruit that will remain. What many may fail to realize is that they don't expect fruit to expose the place in which they govern from. However, that is the purpose of fruit. Fruit and its condition reveals what's in the ground and what's been nourishing the ground that it has been placed in. What we have been seeing in our day, and what we see throughout generations, is the fruit of our impact. Whether our lives and our families have been rooted in the presence of God, in religious activity, or in darkness, we can see the true evidence of God in our life or whether there is some sort of mixture. It is unfortunate, but many will not make attempts to pursue the presence of the Lord, making attempts to govern in their own way. As we can see, this is a costly mistake. Most will try to build and create something in the Earth that did not come from communion with God, and on the day of judgment, it will be revealed.

> 1 Corinthians 3:13-15 states *"Every man's work shall be made manifest: for the day shall declare it, because it shall be revealed by fire; and the fire shall try every man's work of what sort it is. If any man's work abide which he hath built thereupon, he shall receive a reward. If any man's work shall be burned, he shall suffer loss: but he himself shall be saved; yet so as by fire."*

So, what you do with what you have been given through time and space (sphere) of influence will be revealed. The place you've governed from will be revealed. The Scriptures stated that it will be clear, and if we were to be honest, it is clear even now.

Nevertheless, I believe with my whole heart that we still have the opportunity to set some things in their appropriate place. Through moments like this one right now, we have the opportunity to produce new fruit by heeding the word of the Lord and setting our hearts on that which flows out of our time in God's presence. For that is where the Blueprint for transformational governance is revealed, transferred, and entrusted to you.

Transformational governance carries the objective to guard and steward a sphere, space, industry, territory, and more with the sole focus being what God always wanted to see in this realm. True and eternal transformation only comes by way of the presence of the Lord, for He himself is true and eternal. The evidence of true transformation in our governance will flow easily from our position of being established, empowered, and fueled by no one else but the One who IS.

When you set your heart to focus on His presence, when you set your heart to understand what He wants in the Earth through you, when you set your heart to truly value what He is entrusting into your hands, you will lead with power, walk with boldness, and release His transformative power in the Earth.

This is that same power that the 120 vessels in the upper room on the day of Pentecost were baptized with (Acts 2). This is the same power that gave the Apostles boldness to declare God's word as they went (Acts 4). This is the power of God that will transform a world by the strong witness of a few dispatched in regions. The testimony will go before you and be strong and clear; they will testify and say, *"These that have turned the world upside down ..."* (Acts 17:6). In other words, these are the ones who are transforming our world. In the Scriptures, this accusation came from those who were Jews, and they were envious. I could only imagine that the jealousy and anger could have brewed because eternal transformation was happening, and it was shifting cities, changing households and nations, and impacting generations.

As much as many of the world would not like it, this is what we have been entrusted with by God. As His own, it is our heart's desire to bring Him delight in sincerely fulfilling His heart in our stewardship. We won't let the plan of God already fulfilled be in vain. Jesus has already come and completed His assignment to redeem us back to this place. This is a place of Identity, inheritance, authority, and our reasonable service. Our response to the Lord should show our value for this redeemed place and reflect our growth and relationship with God. For we are a people who know our God; we shall be strong, and we shall perform great exploits for Him on the Earth—The place He has founded and established (Daniel 11: 32, Psalms 24:1).

Psalmist Raine is an apostolic voice, author, shepherd, wife, and mother with a passion to empower the Body of Christ with truth through encounters and tools that transform lives, restoring and refreshing one's original God-designed DNA. She is known worldwide as a renowned worship leader, but she is a vessel that God uses to release His heart for the Kingdom. You can learn more and connect via her website at www.berefresh.com.

SECTION VI: HEALING & IDENTITY

20

CHOOSE YOUR IMPACT

Evangelist Tracie L. Vick

"I call heaven and earth to record this day against you, that I have set before you life and death, blessing and cursing: therefore choose life, that both thou and thy seed may live" (Deuteronomy 30:19).

Every day, we are faced with choices that echo far beyond our own lives. The power of impact begins in one simple decision: to choose life, even after death tried to silence you.

The Breaking

There was a time I thought my pain would define me forever. Losing my son to gun violence broke me in ways I can't fully describe. Death had previously struck in my immediate family when I was ten years old. My brother, who was fifteen at the time, went out to play basketball and never returned home. He passed away right on the basketball court. I then lost my father when I was twenty-seven. These were the three most important men in my life—my brother, my father, and my son—and I did not get the chance to grow old with any of them.

My brother's passing left a silence in our home that I was too young to understand, and when my father lost his son, it shattered him. He had a mental breakdown after my brother's death. Years later, when he passed away in Florida, I carried the ache of a relationship that never had time to fully bloom. We only saw each other on short visits, and the distance left questions that life never answered.

And then losing my son—it felt like that loss tried to end me. It was as if the same cycle that broke my father wanted to continue through me. But I refused to let that happen. I chose to fight—for my mind, for my soul, and for my legacy.

In the midst of all of that, I had a mother who did her best to care for me—a resilient woman who worked hard to provide for her children but also one who didn't know how to communicate love. I never heard the words, "I love you." I never heard, "You can do anything you put your mind to." Instead, I heard more of what I could not do. My mother placed her limitations on me.

The message was, "Get one job and keep that job for the rest of your life." Imagine if I had followed that path.

By no means is this to belittle my mother—this is simply my truth. I grew up fighting battles no child should ever have to endure.

I remember stepping between grown men who tried to attack my mother, even fighting my sister's boyfriend at sixteen years old. I carried adult-sized pain in a child's body. You would think that the impact I endured from back when I was a little girl would have broken me completely. My influence could have been destructive as well as detrimental to my children, as I carried buried trauma. My decisions have passed pain straight into my children. And, truthfully, I have made several mistakes that could have shifted the trajectory of their lives. But this isn't about blame—it's about the roadmap that led me to redemption.

Because part of choosing your impact is first choosing God. Then, you choose yourself. That's where power begins—that's how impact is cultivated. I didn't get to choose what happened to me, but I do get to choose what comes from me.

Impact is inevitable. Life leaves marks—some beautiful, some brutal—but the choice of how those marks shape others is ours. The question isn't whether you'll make an impact; it's what kind. Will your impact flow from pain or from purpose, from bitterness or from healing?

The Surrendering

When I finally surrendered my pain to God, I realized my story wasn't punishment—it was preparation. Every tear was a seed. Every loss was an awakening. Every test was shaping my influence.

> *"To appoint unto them that mourn in Zion, to give unto them beauty for ashes, the oil of joy for mourning, the garment of praise for the spirit of heaviness; that they might be called trees of righteousness, the planting of the Lord, that he might be glorified"* (Isaiah 61:3).

When I decided to surrender to God—when I opened up and let Him have rule, reign, and dominion over my life—everything began to change. People often say, "It's not that easy," and they're right. But the same way we can make quick decisions to do wrong, we can also choose God. Both paths are hard, but one leads to ruin, and the other leads to redemption. With God, it may not be easy, but it's better. It's more rewarding. He gives you strength when you have none left. He covers you when you can't cover yourself. He restores what you thought was beyond repair.

When you're out there in the world without Him, you're dangling by yourself—exposed to influences that can lead you down a road you may never recover from.

I didn't want to hear the words, "*I never knew you: depart from me*" (Matthew 7:23). That thought alone became my wake-up call. So, I said, "Enough is enough." My surrender wasn't transactional. It wasn't about what I wanted from God—it was about giving myself fully to Him. I wanted it. I craved it. I needed it. And that's when He started shifting me. He changed me from the inside out.

Now I have daughters. I have grandchildren. What I do, they see. Every move I make, they notice. That's why I have to be intentional about the kind of legacy I leave behind—one that heals, not harms; one that inspires faith, not fear. Legacy isn't built in a moment—it's built in daily choices: how I respond when I'm hurt, how I love when it's hard, and how I forgive when I want revenge.

> *"A good man leaveth an inheritance to his children's children: and the wealth of the sinner is laid up for the just"* (Proverbs 13:22).

The Rewrite

Healing didn't happen overnight. It wasn't one prayer or one service that fixed everything. Healing was—and still is—a process. It's the daily decision to rise, even when you don't feel like rising. It's facing your truth without shame and allowing God to rewrite the parts of your story that once brought life-altering heartache. For me, healing started when I stopped pretending to be okay. I stopped performing and allowed God to strengthen me. I started journaling again, praying again, crying again. There were days I had to forgive myself for the things I did while broken—the people I hurt, the words I spoke in anger, the decisions made from pain.

But with every layer, I surrendered and let God rebuild me. He renewed my faith and my peace of mind.

> *"But the God of all grace, who hath called us unto his eternal glory by Christ Jesus, after that ye have suffered a while, make you perfect, stablish, strengthen, settle you"* (1 Peter 5:10).

Out of that healing, my She Found Her ministry emerged—not just a brand but a movement. A declaration that no matter what life strips away, a woman can rise, heal, and find herself again in God. My pain became a platform, not a prison. What once silenced me now fuels my purpose.

The Legacy

I remember growing up going to church with my mother, aunt, and grandmother. I'd watch people praise God while my family always remained poised and quiet. Years later, that same aunt came to visit me from Alabama and attended church with me in Chicago. During the service, I felt the presence of the Holy Spirit so strongly that I couldn't contain it. I began to cry out, to lift my hands, to shout, "Hallelujah!" I was worshipping freely. But my aunt tugged on my shirt, whispering for me to sit down because I was embarrassing her. That's when I realized how powerful influence truly is. Generational impact can either free you or bind you. Because she didn't know how to express her praise, she tried to quiet mine. But I couldn't—wouldn't—let her influence stop my worship. What my aunt didn't realize is she was tugging at generations of suppressed worship. In that moment, I stood—not just for myself but for every woman in my bloodline who was told to sit down when her soul wanted to stand, when her soul wanted to praise, when her soul longed to worship her Heavenly Father in spirit and in truth. For as the psalmist declared, "*Let every thing that hath breath PRAISE THE LORD. Praise ye the Lord*" (Psalm 150:6).

We have to be careful about what we pass down from generation to generation. Some patterns of silence and suppression are not God. That day, I learned my relationship with Him is personal. It isn't inherited; it's chosen. What God has for me isn't dependent on how anyone else praises Him. It's between me and Him.

> "*And if it seem evil unto you to serve the LORD, choose you this day whom ye will serve; whether the gods which your fathers served that were on the other side of the flood, or the gods of the Amorites, in whose land ye dwell: but as for me and my house, we will serve the LORD*" (Joshua 24:15).

Today, I know that my story could have gone another way. I could have allowed grief, rage, and silence to rule me. But I chose HEALING; I chose GOD! The generational bondage in my family, it ends starting with me. I get to choose whether my influence will be trauma, bondage, resentment, bitterness, confrontation, or stifling, or whether it will be encouragement, love, healing, restoration, and uplifting.

The impact I choose today will echo through my daughters and my grandchildren. Because I chose healing over hurt, they will inherit peace instead of pain, faith instead of fear. My surrender to God didn't just change my story—it rewrote the legacy of everyone connected to me.

I chose my impact—and in doing so, I broke the curse, birthed the change, and chose life for my bloodline.

> "*And we know that all things work together for good to them that love God, to them who are the called according to his purpose*" (Romans 8:28).

SO, CHOOSE YOUR IMPACT!

Tracie is a God Fearing, Woman of God. She is licensed Evangelist, and a current student at Midwest School of Theology. She is an Author of Rewritten, I Am Free, No Longer Bound, the founder of SHE FOUND HER, a healed and whole soul. Tracie is also the founder of Colorism No More. She is a certified Life and Grief Coach. She also works for Second Chance Initiative, Non-Profit Organization aimed at helping to eliminate gun violence.

21

MOM WITH A PLAN

From Hustle to Holy Leadership

Marlo Payne

Milk Money & Grace

I'll never forget the Saturday morning I went digging for milk money, and grace met me on my kitchen floor. My boys were little, and life as a single mom had a way of keeping me on my knees—sometimes in prayer, sometimes in exhaustion. That morning, I emptied every purse, looked in every drawer, and turned over every couch cushion until I found the exact change I needed.

I sat there on the floor with tears streaming down my face—not because we were struggling, but because God had provided again. That morning, I realized I could either focus on what I lacked or surrender completely to the One who never fails to provide. It wasn't just milk money. It was my moment of clarity. My moment of grace.

> "The steps of a good man are ordered by the LORD:
> and he delighteth in his way." (Psalm 37:23).

Even when we don't see the next step, God is already ordering it.

Roots of Perseverance

I grew up poor by today's standards, but we never knew it. My dad worked long hours in a factory with an unmatched work ethic, also picking up odd jobs, while my mom stayed home with us. They carried a quiet strength and a contentment for things that truly mattered.

From a young age, I watched what perseverance looked like. I learned that showing up every day, even when it's hard, is what builds character. I didn't know it then, but God was using those years to teach me how to govern my life with hard work and integrity before ever giving me influence.

Even when life got hard and church attendance faded for a season, the seeds of faith were already in me. I carried them through the years, even when I didn't understand what God was doing with them. Through those early lessons, He was teaching me how to lead with integrity, persevere through uncertainty, and trust His timing even when I couldn't trace His plan.

> "Strength and honour are her clothing; and she shall rejoice in time to come. She openeth her mouth with wisdom; and in her tongue is the law of kindness. She looketh well to the ways of her household, and eateth not the bread of idleness" (Proverbs 31:25-27).

Godly leadership begins at home, where strength and stewardship are first tested.

Hustle vs. Grace

I have worn a lot of hats in my adult years. I worked jobs that paid the bills, chased opportunities that stretched me, and eventually found success as a realtor. I loved the challenge of sales—it was deeply satisfying to help others make life-changing decisions.

What I didn't realize at the time was that each job, each mentor, and each experience was part of my training ground.

Looking back, I can see how God strategically placed mentors in my path—people who saw something in me that I hadn't yet recognized in myself. From Sandy, who encouraged confidence in my modeling and pageant career at a young age, to the many women I met through entrepreneurship; from a successful broker who took me under her wing as I started in real estate, to Deborah, who helped to strengthen my faith; to Lisa and my sister Jamie, who stayed by my side in all seasons; and finally, a husband who became my greatest influence.

But I'll be honest—I wore my hustle like a badge of honor. I thought constant movement equaled progress. I believed being busy meant being productive. I measured my worth by my workload and my identity by what I achieved. Success looked good on the outside, but inside I was running on fumes.

I know now that striving and surrender can't coexist. Hustle kept me moving; grace kept me becoming. The more I tried to control every outcome, the more drained I became.

Yet even in the chaos, God was preparing me to stop leading from pressure and start leading from purpose. The noise of doing it all had begun to drown out the whisper of my calling. God slowed me down in order to set me free.

> "And let us not be weary in well doing: for in due season we shall reap, if we faint not" (Galatians 6:9).

Grace always rewards perseverance.

The Movement: Moms with a Plan

At forty years old, I finally realized my past wasn't a detour—it was preparation. I became my family's first millionaire and broke generational limits that had lingered for years. Every struggle, every stretch, every season of waiting had led me here.

It was one of my mentors—now my business partner and best friend, Heather—who asked me the question that changed everything: "Are you happy?" That question still echoes in my heart today. It's a simple question, but when answered honestly, it can shift your perspective and open your eyes to what could be.

Together with a few friends, we started a community called Moms with a Plan—a movement born from the tension between faith, success, and hustle in the home-based business world. We were women trying to do it all while quietly wondering if there was more. Together, we built a community centered on faith-based mentorship, connection, and income resources.

We discovered that we could turn everyday expenses into everyday income while keeping our hearts grounded in what matters most: faith, family, and freedom. Moms with a Plan became more than a name—it became a movement. A safe place for women to rediscover confidence, lead their homes well, and walk out their calling without the constant grind.

Hundreds of women have been coached.

Hundreds of families are paying off debt.

Hundreds of small businesses have launched.

Lives are being changed, and legacies are being written.

Generational Impact

Today, I see the fruit of choosing grace over grind. My children, nieces, and the women I mentor live with a sense of peace, purpose, and provision that I never knew at their age.

They steward their homes with strength and joy. They know that God's plan isn't something to chase—it's something to trust.

Emma, my best friend's daughter, recently reached out to share how I've inspired her to choose entrepreneurship. It was a full-circle moment—knowing she has chosen to lead from faith, not fear.

The values I learned around that kitchen table—work hard, be kind, and trust God—became the same principles I now lead others with.

You don't have to hustle for what grace has already given you. That truth became my legacy, and it's the one I hope every woman who hears my story carries forward, especially my beautiful daughter, Liv.

The Call to Action

Grace has a way of meeting you between who you were and who God is calling you to be. It shows up when you're ready to quit, when the plan falls apart, or when the doors you wanted to open stay shut.

So remember, our plan is not always our plan. Put the word YET behind every effort and dream.

I'm not there—yet.

The door hasn't opened—yet.

The plan isn't clear—yet.

> "A man's heart deviseth his way: but the LORD directeth his steps" (Proverbs 16:9).

Prayer & Charge for Moms

> Lord, thank You for the gift of grace that meets us in the middle—between our plans and Your purpose. Teach us to lead from peace, to trust Your timing, and to rest in the truth that we are already equipped for the calling You've placed within us.

May every mom reading this rise with renewed confidence, build with integrity, and walk in holy leadership—not from hustle, but from grace.

Amen.

You don't have to hustle for what grace has already given you.

Marlo Payne is a mentor, business coach, and entrepreneur who helps women and moms build confidence, financial freedom, and healthier homes through a sustainable wellness company. She leads Moms With a Plan, a thriving community empowering women to dream bigger and step into their God-given purpose. With nearly a decade of leadership experience, Marlo blends heart, hope, and practical tools. She lives on Sunset Ranch in Illinois, where she continues inspiring women to rise in faith and freedom.

22

LEGACY IMPACTING A GENERATION

Kimberly L. McClinton

At the age of sixteen, my life changed forever. I was young, full of dreams, and in the middle of what was supposed to be a carefree season of high school. Then, in what felt like a single moment, everything shifted—I found out I was pregnant.

When I shared the news with my family, the atmosphere in my world changed overnight. What had been laughter, plans, and youthful freedom quickly transformed into serious conversations, tears, and uncertainty. It was not a part of my plan, nor my parents' vision for me. I suddenly had to face decisions that were far beyond my years.

But life has a way of accelerating when God has a purpose for you. Within four months, I went from being a junior in high school to a wife, a graduate, and a college student—all while expecting my first child. In April, I was attending high school classes. By June, I had finished my junior year, entered summer school to complete English IV and qualified for graduation. By July, I was married. By August, I was walking onto a college campus, carrying not just books but also the weight of a new life inside me.

It was a whirlwind—a breathtaking, confusing, transformative season that took me from adolescence to adulthood almost overnight. I did not have a roadmap, but I had faith. I did not have all the answers, but I had a sense, deep within my soul, that God was not finished with me yet.

Learning to Stand in Faith

As I tried to navigate college, marriage, and the looming reality of motherhood, I quickly realized that I could not rely on my own strength. I was living in the consequences of my choices, but I was also standing at the beginning of something sacred—a chance to rewrite the story for the generations that would follow me.

I remember praying with a desperation I had never known before. I prayed for my life, yes, but even more fervently, I prayed for my child. I asked God to protect this baby from the pain I had endured, to give them a life filled with purpose, faith, and strength. I declared that the generational curses—the cycles of brokenness, fear, and struggle—would end with me. This child, I promised God, would be dedicated to Him.

Prayer was not new to me. I had been raised to call on the name of the Lord. My family carried a long, proud lineage of ministers, worshippers, and spiritual leaders. Calling on God's name was as natural to me as breathing. But up until that point, prayer had been more of a family tradition than a personal necessity. It was part of our heritage, something we did out of reverence and rhythm.

It wasn't until I was sixteen, alone in my room, my heart heavy with uncertainty, that I experienced what it meant to truly need Him—not because I had been told so, but because my very survival depended on it.

Understanding Legacy

The word "legacy" doesn't appear in the Bible in its English form, but its meaning is woven through the Word from Genesis to Revelation. A biblical legacy is more than money or property—it's the passing down of faith, values, and moral courage. It's what we leave in the hearts of our children long after we're gone.

The Bible gives us many examples:

- Deuteronomy 6:6-7 reminds us, *"And these words, which I command thee this day, shall be in thine heart. And thou shalt teach them diligently unto thy children, and shalt talk of them when thou sittest in thine house, and when thou walkest by the way, and when thou liest down, and when thou risest up."*

  Legacy begins with teaching. It is the consistent repetition of truth and love that plants God's word deep within a child's heart.

- Proverbs 13:22 says, *"A good man leaveth an inheritance to his children's children."*

True inheritance extends beyond wealth — it's the spiritual and moral compass we pass through generations.

- 2 Timothy 1:5 speaks of Timothy's faith that lived first in his grandmother Lois and his mother Eunice and now lived in him.

  Faith is generational when it is lived authentically and modeled daily.

These Scriptures remind me that legacy is not just what we leave behind but what we live out daily.

When I think about the word "inheritance," I am reminded that it's not just something you hold—it's something that's *in here.* It lives within us. A good legacy is planted so deep that it becomes a part of your DNA. My faith, though challenged by circumstance, was already *in me.* It took this life-changing experience for me to realize how real and powerful that legacy was.

Impacting a Generation

From that moment forward, I became determined—fiercely determined—to ensure that the next generation in my family would rise above every limitation that had held us back. I wanted my children to know that they were not accidents or victims of circumstance, but divine assignments. I wanted them to believe that their dreams mattered and that they were worthy of living a full, abundant life.

In my home, I made sure that faith was not a Sunday event but a daily conversation. My children heard prayer. They saw faith in motion. They knew right from wrong, and they understood that the world outside might whisper lies, but home was the place where truth resided.

A Heritage of Greatness

My passion for legacy is rooted in the example set by those before me. On my grandfather's deathbed, he told me, "We have to have at least one star in the family—someone to carry the family name and legacy on."

My grandparents were remarkable. My grandfather appeared on the cover of *Jet* magazine, and my grandmother was a pioneer—one of the first female gospel radio hosts, a national singer, an emcee, and an etiquette coach. She inspired others to find their voice and use it well. My grandfather created jobs for friends and family. Together, they modeled creativity, generosity, and leadership.

My parents continued that legacy, encouraging us to pursue education and creative expression. And, even further back, our lineage includes builders, porters, and church organizers who helped establish ministries in the early Church of God in Christ movement. Our family tree, traced back to the 1700s, is full of both triumphs and trials—faith and flaws. Prayer and leadership run deep in our veins, but so do certain vices that have tried to undermine our progress.

Breaking the Cycle

Through my own experiences, I learned something powerful: Legacies don't only carry blessings—they can also carry burdens. The Bible instructs us to pass down godly wisdom, but if we are not intentional, we can also pass down patterns of pain.

In my family, two of those recurring struggles were early pregnancies and addictions. These vices had silently followed generations before me, cutting short dreams and distorting destinies. When I found myself following the same path of early pregnancy, I knew immediately that this could not continue. I had to become the line in the sand—the one who said, "This ends with me."

It wasn't easy. Transformation rarely is. But I learned that breaking generational curses begins with awareness, repentance, and replacement. You must first recognize the pattern, then renounce it, and finally replace it with God's truth.

So, I began to speak differently in my home. I taught my children that distractions can derail destiny, but focus leads to fulfillment. I reminded them that leadership is in our DNA—but it's up to each of us to decide which direction we will lead.

The Scripture in Proverbs 22:6 became my anchor: *"Train up a child in the way he should go: and when he is old, he will not depart from it."* Training is not a one-time act—it is the consistent nurturing of faith, the daily reinforcement of values, the gentle correction when the path grows unclear.

Living the Legacy

Over the years, I've watched my children grow into capable, thoughtful, purpose-driven individuals. They know the story. They know where we've come from and what we've overcome. They understand that their talents are not random—they are divine deposits meant to bless others.

They also know the vices that once hindered our family, and because of that awareness, they walk with discernment. Awareness is not fear; it's power. When you know what tried to break your family, you can better guard what God is building through you.

When I see them leading, achieving, and loving others well, I am reminded that every prayer I prayed was worth it. Every tear I cried became a seed in the soil of their future.

The Weight and Wonder of Legacy

Legacy is not about perfection; it's about persistence. It's choosing to keep walking, keep believing, and keep sowing, even when life feels unfair or uncertain. It's about understanding that your story—no matter how messy—can become a manual for someone else's victory.

When I look back, I see that the sixteen-year-old girl who once felt afraid and unprepared was, in fact, the beginning of something sacred. God took my fear and turned it into faith. He took my mistakes and used them as a message.

And so, I live now with a heart full of gratitude and conviction. My purpose is clear: to continue pouring into the next generation—not just my children, but everyone I meet. To remind them that God can take what seems like a detour and use it as a divine direction.

I will continue to share my story because someone needs to hear it—someone who feels like their life has gone off-course, someone who fears they have disappointed God or their family. To you, I say this: There is still destiny in your story. God is not done with you.

Leaving More Than Memories

As long as I live, I will invest in building a lasting legacy of believers who will lead with integrity, serve with compassion, and live with faith. My goal is not just to be remembered, but to be *reflected*—in the faith of my children, in the love of my grandchildren, and in the lives of all who are influenced by our family's testimony.

A true legacy is not measured by earthly success but by eternal impact. It's measured by the hearts you heal, the lives you inspire, and the faith you awaken in others.

When I pray now, I thank God for trusting me with this story—for allowing me to live long enough to see the fruit of the seeds I once planted in tears. I thank Him for the generations before me, who carried faith even when they faltered, and for the generations after me, who will take it even further.

Because that's what legacy is—it's faith that outlives us. It's love that multiplies. It's the echo of God's promises through our lives, resonating long after our voices are gone.

And as for me and my house—we will continue to serve the Lord.

Apostle Kimberly L. McClinton, PhD, is a dedicated servant leader with over 30 years in ministry and philanthropy. Founder of Life in Christ Family Worship Center International and Pure Life Network, she empowers churches and communities, serves as an educator, author, and musician, and leads outreach worldwide. She resides in Chicagoland with her husband, children, and grandchildren.

kimberlylmcclinton.com
kmcclinton@licfwc.org

23

THE IMPACT I WANT TO MAKE ON THIS GENERATION

Alexis Lowry

"Even though I grew up in church, I had to learn that knowing *about* God isn't the same as knowing Him."

I am part of Generation Z those born between 1997 and 2012. Yes, it's a wide age range, but within this generation are world changers, Kingdom influencers, and young people filled with the Holy Spirit. There are also many who have yet to experience a true encounter with Jesus. And when I say *encounter*, I'm talking about the kind that changes your life forever not a moment, but an entrance into eternity.

I've been in church my whole life. I was baptized when I was old enough to understand what I was doing, and people often called me a "church kid." That label came with assumptions that my life was easy, that my "oil was cheap," that I had nothing to struggle through. But like CeCe Winans sings in *Alabaster Box*, "You don't know the cost of the oil in my alabaster box." My oil was produced through crushing and pressing, and its fragrance is a testimony to the grace and mercy of God.

The Hidden Battles Behind the Church Kid Smile

I've faced depression and anxiety especially after being diagnosed with scoliosis in 2019. I wore a hard plastic back brace for twenty-two hours a day, stretching from my neck to my hips. I had to relearn how to pick things up, how to dress, how to sleep. And every night, the enemy whispered lies that I wouldn't be able to breathe or survive the night.

Even when fear tried to fog my prayers and drown my faith, something inside me refused to let go of God.

People assume that growing up in church means immunity from struggle. But the truth is, sometimes the ones raised around the things of God fight the deepest battles because the enemy tries hardest to silence the voices God wants to use.

I didn't always know how to say,

"Hey, I know God is real, but everything feels heavy."

Faith and struggle can live in the same body. Faith doesn't remove the fight, faith helps you survive it.

When Life Shifted Overnight

That scoliosis diagnosis changed everything. One appointment flipped my entire routine, my confidence, my comfort. The brace squeezed me in ways I didn't know could hurt. Picking anything up became a strategy. Sleeping became a negotiation. Feeling normal became a prayer.

But the hardest part wasn't the physical limitation, it was the thoughts.

The enemy rarely shouts. He whispers.

Just like in Genesis, when Eve heard, "Did God really say?"

For me, the whispers sounded like:

What if you can't breathe?

What if something goes wrong?

What if you don't make it through the night?

Fear felt loud. Fear felt real. But God was louder.

My prayers didn't always sound spiritual. Sometimes they were just, "God, please help me make it through tonight." Yet God heard me. Even when my faith felt small, God stayed close.

Spiritual warfare doesn't always look dramatic. Sometimes it's a quiet fog over the mind, making you doubt your worth, your identity, your voice, your prayers.

But those hidden battles became holy ground — because that's where God began shaping me.

Encounter Over Aesthetic: Meeting Jesus for Myself

Growing up in church teaches you many things, but it cannot teach you to *know* God for yourself. You can know songs, sermons, and Scriptures, and still not know His voice.

For years, I thought encountering God meant tears, shaking, falling out at the altar — and sometimes that does happen. But my real encounter came quietly.

It wasn't during a service.

It wasn't emotional or loud.

It was a late night where fear tried to convince me I was alone.

My thoughts raced. My heart felt heavy. Prayer felt foggy. And I asked myself:

Why does my mind feel like a war zone?

Why does prayer feel like pushing through mud?

Why do I feel far from God even though I'm trying?

Then I realized:

The enemy wasn't attacking my body, he was attacking my identity.

He wanted me to believe my prayers were weak.

That my faith was fake.

That my voice didn't matter.

That doubt disqualified me.

But that night, I whispered "Jesus."

Not as a church kid.

Not as someone trying to look spiritual.

But as a daughter calling out to her Father.

And something shifted.

Not dramatically. Not instantly.

But peace came slow, steady, undeniable.

It told me:

"You're not fighting alone."

That's when I understood: encounters with God are not performances. They are invitations to freedom, truth, intimacy, and healing.

When I recognized His presence, the lies began losing their power. Freedom didn't come all at once. It came like morning light, gradual, gentle, but unstoppable.

A Mess Made Into a Masterpiece

Christmas is my favorite season: the lights, the treats, the parties, the JOY. But I will never forget the reason for the season. Jesus came not in a palace but in a manger a feeding trough. What looked like a mess was divine strategy.

God still works the same way today.

He takes our ashes and makes them beautiful (Isaiah 61:3).

He takes what feels unusable and turns it into purpose.

When I was diagnosed with scoliosis, I asked,

"How can God use this?"

The Calling on Gen Z: Carriers of the Light

If there's one thing I know about my generation, it's this: **Gen Z wants something real.**

We don't hide our questions.

We don't want shallow religion.

We want authenticity, purpose, truth.

People see Gen Z and think of chaos, confusion, rebellion.

God sees revivalists. He sees:

- worship leaders
- intercessors
- prophets and pastors
- missionaries and evangelists
- entrepreneurs
- bold teenagers carrying fire into places older generations can't reach

He sees courage rising in classrooms, group chats, locker rooms, youth groups, social media everywhere.

I used to underestimate my generation. But now I see why darkness fights us so fiercely. Anxiety, identity confusion, suicide, or even pressure, but where darkness increases, light shines even brighter.

Jesus said, "You are the light of the world." Not later. Not when you're older. Right now.

He's not talking to the flawless — He's talking to the willing.

Look at Mary Magdalene. Oppressed, bound, tormented — yet she became the first preacher of the Resurrection. God uses the unexpected.

We Are Not Disconnected — We Are Desperate

Gen Z doesn't want religion without relationship. We want the real Jesus. And He is using young people **right now**:

- the quiet girl praying in the bathroom stall
- the athlete leading a locker room Bible study
- the student posting Scriptures online
- the teen worshipping privately because they're shy publicly
- the one choosing purity and integrity in a culture that mocks it

God sees all of it. And He sees you.

Somewhere between my braces, my battles, my prayers, and my breakthroughs, I realized:

This generation is not forgotten.

We are appointed.

We are anointed.

We are called.

That's why I refuse to stay silent.

If God turned my pain into purpose — imagine what He will do through an entire generation saying "yes."

A revival is not coming. **It has already started — inside of us**

Daughter of the King Alexis Rosa Lowry, 16, is a distinguished servant leader and opera vocalist whose faith and academic excellence underpin her success. As the inaugural Miss Indigenous North Carolina Ambassador, her platform, “Challenge Your Challenges,” empowers others to overcome adversity. A published author and aspiring orthodontist, Alexis exemplifies leadership, service, and resilience.

24

RE-MEMBERING A GENERATION

The Mandate to Govern, Build, and Impact

Dr. Deborah C. Anthony

One generation shall praise thy works to another, and shall declare thy mighty acts" (Psalm 145:4).

There are certain moments in history when God does more than speak—He summons. He summons a people to attention. He summons a generation to responsibility. He summons the Body of Christ to remember who she is, what she carries, and why she exists. As I reflect on the weight of this anthology, Graced to Govern – Impacting a Generation (Series Two), I am reminded that impact is not a casual idea. It is a calling. It is a mandate. It is a sacred trust that each generation must steward with intentionality, humility, and courage.

When I think about the transition between Joshua's generation and the one that followed, I am always gripped by the chilling verse in Judges 2:10. After Joshua died, Scripture records that an entirely new generation arose—one that "knew not the LORD, nor yet the works which he had done for Israel." This is not merely a story from ancient history; it is a warning for every age. How does a generation grow up unaware of the God who delivered their parents? How does a people lose sight of miracles so monumental they should have shaped their Identity forever? It happens slowly, almost imperceptibly. It happens when remembrance becomes optional rather than essential. It happens when stories go untold, when wisdom is not transferred, and when generational disconnection becomes normalized. Forgetfulness does not happen in a moment; it happens through neglect.

That is why this anthology exists. It exists to confront forgetfulness. It exists to repair the break in memory. It exists so we do not become the generation that loses sight of the God who has carried us through wilderness, war, deliverance, healing, revival, and restoration. Impact requires intentional remembrance. You cannot impact the future if you ignore the past. You cannot build for tomorrow if you dishonor yesterday. And you cannot steward generational responsibility if you do not understand the God who guided those before you.

The Mandate to Impact: Why We Cannot Be Passive

Impact is often reduced to a buzzword—something we associate with influence, social change, or inspirational leadership. But in the Kingdom, impact carries far deeper significance. To impact a generation is to alter its trajectory. It means making choices that ripple beyond your lifetime. It means disrupting cycles of spiritual decline. It means standing between what is and what could be and refusing to accept anything less than God's intended future. Impact requires conviction; it requires courage; and it requires a willingness to step into the uncomfortable places where transformation begins.

We live in a time when passivity is easy, and silence is socially acceptable. Yet God has never advanced His Kingdom through passive people. Every major movement of God required men and women who were willing to confront culture, challenge complacency, and awaken the hearts of those around them. When God called His people to remember in Deuteronomy 32:7—"Remember the days of old, consider the years of many generations"—He was commanding them to live with historical awareness. Memory, in Scripture, is not nostalgia; it is governance. Remembering what God has done equips us to govern what God is doing now and to steward what He desires to do next.

To impact a generation, we must be present, awake, and engaged. We must recognize that our silence creates space for spiritual amnesia. When we withhold testimony, we withhold truth. When we shrink back in fear, doubt, or insecurity, we unintentionally contribute to the erosion of faith in the generations that come after us. Impact is a choice—one that demands we stand up and speak out, even when doing so costs us something.

The 2025 Word of the Lord: "I Will Re-Member My Body"

At the beginning of 2025, as I sought God concerning the direction of the Body of Christ, I heard Him speak a word that cut through every distraction:

"I am going to Re-Member My Body."

The weight of that statement rested on me immediately. This was not about recalling memories; it was about reassembling parts. The Body of Christ, across generations, has lived dismembered for far too long. We have seen wisdom trapped in one generation and innovation isolated in another. We have seen the zeal of the young misunderstood and the experience of the seasoned overlooked. We have seen fragmentation, division, and a loss of generational unity that weakens the strength of the Ecclesia.

When God says He will Re-Member the Body, He is talking about joining what has been separated. He is talking about reconnecting voices, gifts, insights, and stories so the Church can stand upright again—whole, complete, strengthened, and aligned. Ephesians 4:16 reminds us that increase only comes when the Body is fitly joined together. Without joining, there is no increase. Without increase, there is no governance. Without governance, there is no impact.

This word awakened me to the reality that every generation has a part to play in preparing the way of the Lord. Not one is disposable. Not one is unnecessary. Not one can be ignored. When the Body is dismembered, the Kingdom is weakened. But when the Body is re-membered, the Kingdom advances with force.

My Assignment: A Builder in the Earth

As I look back on my life, I now understand why God placed me in certain roles, spaces, and seasons. There has always been a builder's anointing on my life. Not in the natural sense of hammer and nails but in the spiritual and governmental sense of structure, systems, legacy, and formation. I come from builders—practical and prophetic. My grandfather, Rev. Hiram Crawford, was a man who built with both his hands and his voice. He built altars. He built churches. He built families. He built convictions. He built courage in those around him. And without even realizing it, he built for me.

I now carry that same mantle. I am called to raise foundations that future generations can stand on. I am called to repair breaches, restore paths, and create structures that support the movement of God in people, communities, and nations. Isaiah 58:12 is not just a verse in my Bible; it is the Blueprint of my life. Being a builder means understanding that impact is not measured only by what you do—but by what remains after you are gone. Builders think in generations, not moments. Their work becomes architecture that outlives them.

This building assignment is why God has positioned me to connect generations. Builders do not work with stones that refuse to touch. Builders gather, align, and assemble. Builders see the value of every piece, no matter how old or new. Builders understand that legacy requires collaboration. And builders know that unity is not optional—it is foundational.

What Impact Truly Means

If we are going to impact a generation, we must reclaim the true meaning of the word "impact." Impact is not simply influence, visibility, or popularity. It is the mark that obedience leaves on time. Impact is the manifestation of fruit that remains, as Jesus described in John 15:16. Impact is what happens when purpose collides with assignment. It is what happens when God's word becomes a hammer that reshapes culture, family, Identity, and destiny.

Impact means building what God reveals, not what people prefer. It means creating systems, writing books, forming institutions, and discipling lives in a way that produces generational continuity. Impact is architectural. It creates pathways where none existed before. It establishes structures that help others succeed. It pushes back against darkness with stability and truth.

Impact is also deeply relational. It requires seeing the value in every generation and recognizing that no one carries the full picture alone. This chapter is not about me making statements; it is about inviting every reader into the realization that they, too, have a part in this generational construction. Whether you are young with fire or seasoned with wisdom, you are a brick in God's building. And every brick matters.

Introducing the Twelve Realms of Influence

If we are going to talk about generational impact, we must talk about where impact is needed. Kingdom influence is not limited to the Church; it extends into every place where decisions are made, stories are shaped, and culture evolves. The Twelve Realms of Influence represent these strategic territories. They consist of faith, family, education, government, business, media, arts, science and technology, law, health, community structures, and global impact. These realms shape how people live, think, believe, and behave.

When we abandon these realms, we leave them vulnerable to voices that do not honor God. When we refuse to engage them, we give permission for ungodly structures to define society. But when we step into our rightful place within these realms—when we govern with grace, integrity, and spiritual authority—we become agents of transformation.

This chapter is an invitation for every reader to discover where they are called to govern. You are not called to all twelve realms, but you are called to one ... or two ... or three. Each realm requires builders. Each realm requires reformers. Each realm requires those willing to stand in the gap and create impact that alters the spiritual and social landscape.

A Call to This Generation

We cannot discuss impact without discussing surrender. Second Chronicles 7:14 is not a gentle verse—it is a divine ultimatum. God promises healing, but only after His people humble themselves, pray, seek His face, and turn from their ways. Before we can impact outwardly, transformation must begin inwardly. Impact begins in the heart before it ever touches the world.

The question we must all ask ourselves is simple:

"Am I His people?"

Am I one who will humble myself?

Am I one who will seek His face?

Am I one who will turn when He convicts me?

Am I one who will allow my life to be used as a bridge for the next generation?

God is calling us beyond passivity into purpose. Beyond silence into stewardship. Beyond comfort into conviction. We cannot be spectators in a world crying out for memory, leadership, and direction. We must be builders. We must be carriers of truth. We must be voices that legacy can depend on.

Conclusion: Prepare the Way

Every part of this chapter points to one truth:

Impact is generational stewardship.

Impact is governance.

Impact is legacy.

Impact is remembrance.

When John the Baptist cried, "Prepare ye the way of the Lord" (Matthew 3:3), he was not speaking to individuals alone—he was speaking to a generation. The same cry echoes now. We are a generation called to prepare. Called to build. Called to remember. Called to Re-Member the Body of Christ. Called to take our place in the realms of influence. Called to create impact that time cannot erase.

I write this chapter not as one who has completed the work but as one fully surrendered to the work still ahead. My prayer is that as you turn these pages, something awakens in you—a recognition of your own assignment, your own realm, your own responsibility to impact the generation God entrusted to you. May you find your place in the Blueprint. May you honor the generations before you. May you build for the generations after you. And may you govern the space God has given you with grace, courage, and conviction.

This is our moment.

This is our call.

This is our impact.

Dr. Deborah C Anthony has dedicated her life to serving the Lord with joy. She shares over 24 years of marriage with her husband, John Anthony, and cherishes their six children, including a son now with the Lord, and her grandson. Combining corporate success with Kingdom purpose, Deborah leads iEmerge Academy, a leadership development program advancing leaders and organizations. As the author of six devotionals and leadership books, her faith-driven words inspire countless lives. Through her unwavering dedication to faith, family, and leadership, Deborah's journey continues to empower generations.

Discover more at
www.deborahcanthony.com.

Grace To Govern is a growing body of voices centered on leadership, purpose, faith, and lasting impact. **Grace to Govern: Impacting A Generation** is the second installment in this collection. .

If you've been inspired by the voices and wisdom in **Grace to Govern: Impacting A Generation**, don't miss the powerful foundation laid in the first volume I of this transformational anthology series.

www.gracedtogovern.com
email: gracedtogovern@gmail.com

Available on Amazon.com

www.ingramcontent.com/pod-product-compliance
Lightning Source LLC
LaVergne TN
LVHW020042110826
845155LV00029B/607